Computer Architecture Lecture Note

Taeho Jo

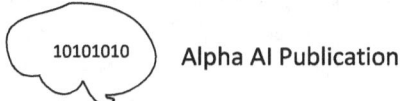

Alpha AI Publication

Computer Architecture: Lecture Note

Copyright © 2024 Alpha AI Publication

All rights reserved by publisher, Alpha AI Publication. No part of this publication may be reproduced or transmitted in any form by any means, electronic, mechanical, photocopying, recording, or otherwise without prior written permission of the publisher.

About Author, Taeho Jo, President of Alpha AI Publication

The author of this book, Taeho Jo, is the founder of the publishing company, Alpha AI Publication, to which the copyright of this book belongs. His specialty is artificial intelligence; he got his Bachelor from Korea University, his Master from POSTECH (Pohang University of Science and Technology), and PhD from University of Ottawa. He has careers in both industrial organizations, Samsung SDS, ETRI (Electronic and Telecommunication Research Institute), and KISTI (Korea Institute of Science and Technology Information) and academic organizations, Inha University and Hongik University as a professor. He has published more than 200 research papers in journals and proceedings, and three books on text mining, machine learning, and deep learning under the contract with the publishing company, Springer, and awarded three times in Marquis Who's Who in the World. The author of this book, Taeho Jo, has a very strong vision for the future as a pioneer of artificial intelligence.

Computer Architecture
Lecturer: Taeho Jo

Contents

- Lecture 1 Introduction---------------------------------------3
- Lecture 2 Data Representation------------------------------30
- Lecture 3 Digital Components-------------------------------57
- Lecture 4 Arithmetic Logic Unit----------------------------86
- Lecture 5 Instruction Set----------------------------------113
- Lecture 6 Instruction Strategies---------------------------143
- Lecture 7 Instruction Execution----------------------------170
- Lecture 8 Control Signal-----------------------------------209

Introduction
Lecture 01

Contents

- Overview
- Computer Organization
- Instruction Execution Cycle
- Related Areas
- Summary and Further Discussions

Overview

- Definition of Computer Architecture
    - Area dealing with the process of executing instructions (program) in hardware level
    - Instruction: elementary unit of program as a word (8, 16, 32, or 64 bits)
    - Instruction = Operation Code + Operands + Conditional Bits
    - Focus on instruction execution cycle:
        - Instruction Fetch
        - Instruction Specification
        - Instruction Execution
        - Instruction Finalization

Overview

- Components in Von Neumann's Computer

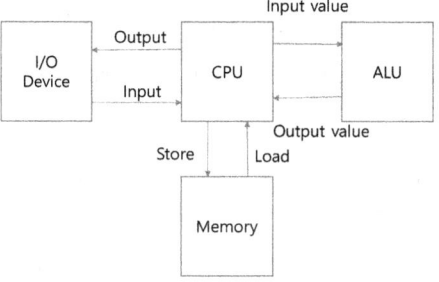

Overview

- Instruction Execution Cycle

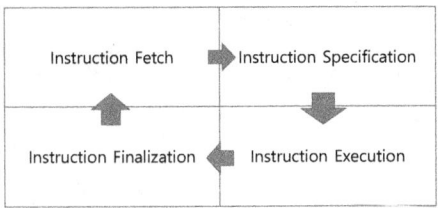

Overview

- Computer Design

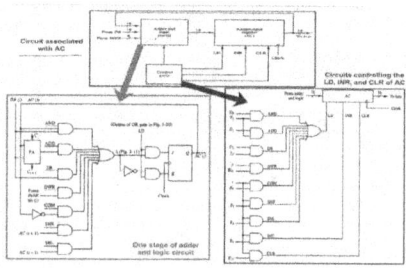

Overview

- Goals of this Lecture
    - Understand concepts of computer organization, architecture and design and their differences
    - Understand components of computer by approaching to them hierarchically
    - Understand process of executing instructions in CPU in abstract view
    - Understand subjects which are related with computer architecture
        - Digital Logic Design
        - Operating System
        - Assembly Programming
        - Embedded System

Computer Organization

- Overview of Computer Organization
    - Area focusing on functions and relations of components in computer
    - Components in computer
        - CPU, ALU, Memory, and I/O Devices
    - CPU: Registers + Control Signal Generator + Cache Memory
    - Single Processor: Multiple CPUs called Cores

Computer Organization

- Motherboard

Computer Organization
- Two Views of Computer

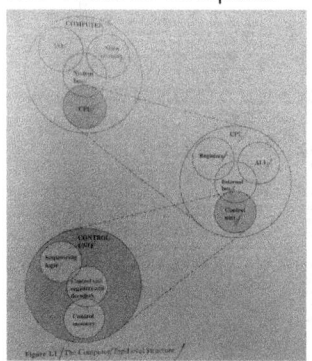
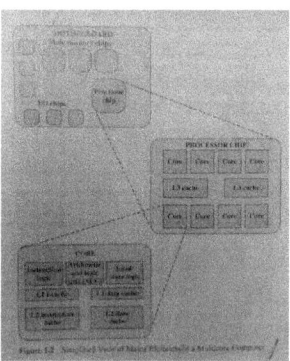

Computer Organization

- Core

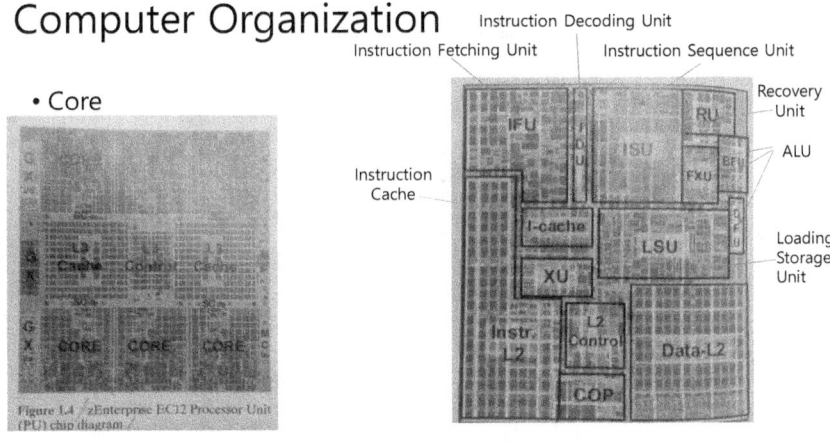

Figure 1.4 zEnterprise BC12 Processor Unit (PU) chip diagram

Computer Organization

- Computer Organization vs Architecture

	Computer Organization	Computer Architecture
Focus	Components	Instruction Execution
What is studied	Structure and Relation	Execution Process
View	Hierarchical View of Computer	Flow of Instruction Execution
Keywords	CPU, ALU, I/O Device, ..	Instruction Set Instruction Format Instruction Programming

Instruction Execution Cycle

- Overview of Instruction Execution
    - Instruction Fetch
        - Take instruction from memory
        - Increment program counter
    - Instruction Specification
        - Decode operation code in instruction
        - Store operands into input registers
    - Instruction Execution
        - Execute operation by control signals and operation code in ALU
        - Store results into output register
    - Instruction Finalization
        - Store value of output register into memory or register file

Instruction Execution Cycle

• Instruction Fetch

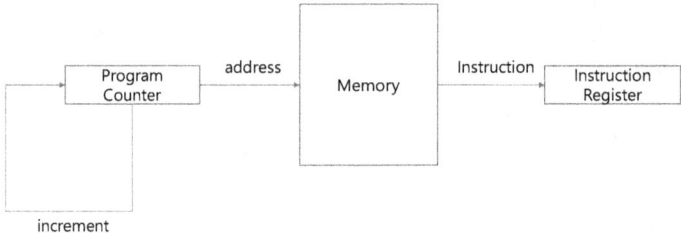

Instruction Execution Cycle

• Instruction Specification

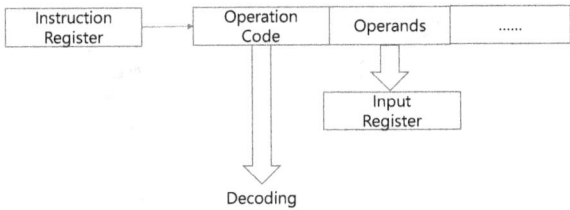

Instruction Execution Cycle

• Instruction Execution

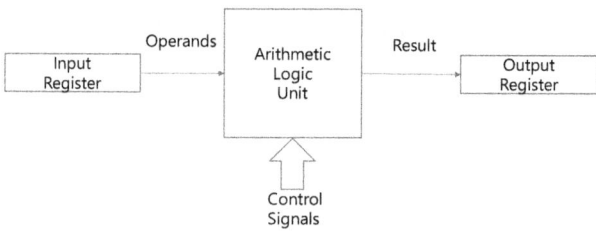

Instruction Execution Cycle

• Instruction Finalization

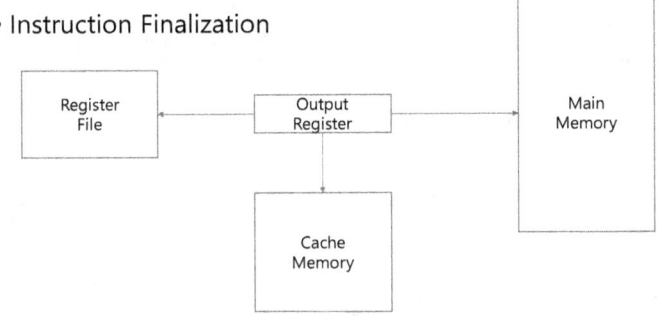

Related Areas
- Overview of Related Areas

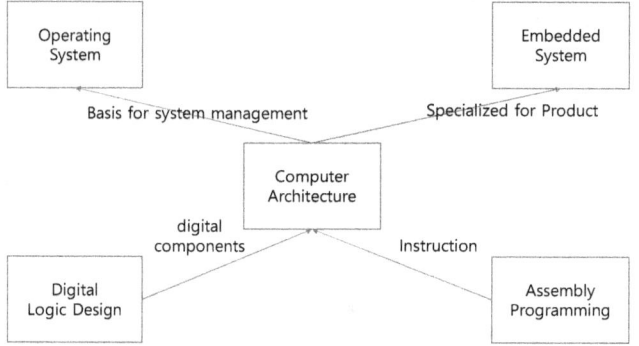

Related Areas

- Digital Logic Design
    - Area for implementing digital components using logic gates
    - Logic gates: AND-gate, OR-gate, XOR-gate, inverter
    - Combinatorial and sequential logic circuits
    - Prerequisite area for studying computer architecture

Related Areas

- Assembly Programming
  - Instruction (Machine Code) → Symbolic Code called Assembly Code
  - Assembler: mapper from Assembly code into Machine Code
  - Intended initially to obtain programming skill of implementing a program by Assembly code
  - Intended recently to understand process of executing program in hardware level

Related Areas

- Operating Systems
    - System program for managing programs in memory and system resources
    - Intermediate level between application program and hardware
    - Focus on strategies of allocating system resources to application programs
    - Computer architecture → Prerequisite for studying Operating System

Related Areas

- Embedded Systems
    - Computer system embedded in particular product
    - Compound of hardware and software specialized for particular purpose
    - Examples of Embedded System
        - Navigator in Automobile
        - Hardware, Software in Mobile Phone
    - Require knowledge about computer architecture for studying Embedded System

Summary and Further Discussions

- Summary
    - Computer architecture: area of computer hardware for studying process of executing instruction
    - Computer: ALU + CPU + Memory + I/O Devices
    - Instruction Execution Cycle
        - Instruction Fetch → Specification → Execution → Finalization
    - Related Areas
        - Digital Logic Design
        - Assembly Programming
        - Operation System
        - Embedded System

Summary and Further Discussions

- CPU Hz

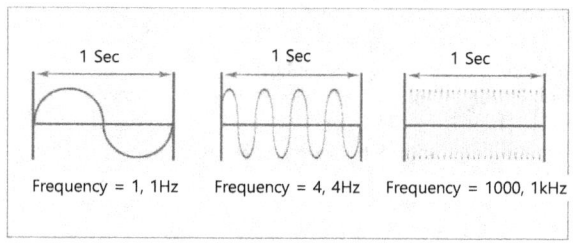

Summary and Further Discussions

Instruction Cycle with Interrupts

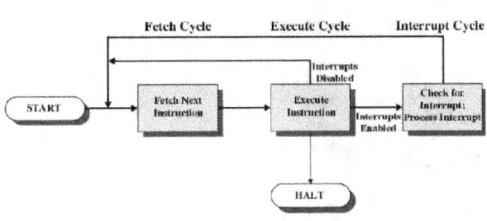

Summary and Further Discussions

- IAS Computer

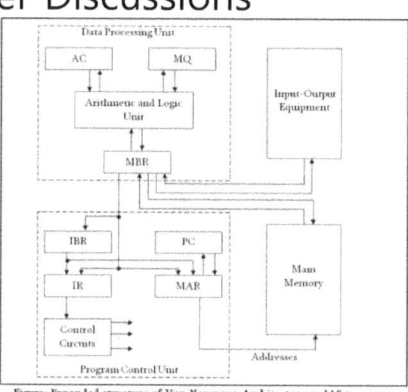

Figure: Expanded structure of Von Neumann Architecture or IAS computer

Summary and Further Discussions
• Instruction Set

Instruction Type	Operations
Data Transfer	Mov, Load, Store, Input, Output
Data Operation	Add, Sub, AND, OR, XOR, Rshift, Lshift, Neg, Inc
Control Transfer	Jump, Skip, Call, Return EQZBranch, NEQZBranch, GTZBranch, LTZBranch EQZRBranch, NEQRBranch, GTRBranch, LTRBranch

Data Representation

Lecture 02

Contents

- Introduction
- Integer Representation
- Operations on Integers
- Float Number Representation
- Operations on Float Numbers

Introduction

- Primitive Data Types
    - Integer: Signed and Unsigned
    - Fixed Point Number: Integer + Faction
    - Float Point Number: Significand + Exponent
    - Character → Integer by ASCII Code

Introduction

- Decimal Numbers

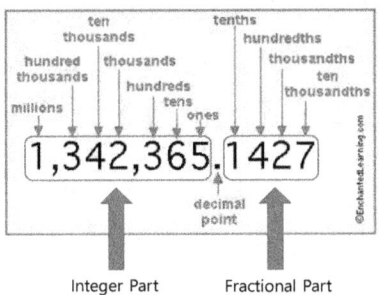

Integer Part   Fractional Part

Introduction

- Decimal ←→ Binary Numbers

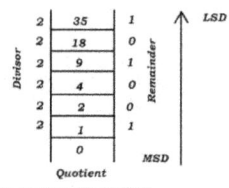
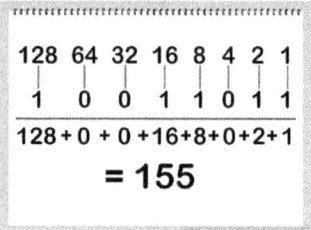

Introduction

- Character with ASCII Code

Dec	Hx	Oct	Char		Dec	Hx	Oct	Html	Chr	Dec	Hx	Oct	Html	Chr	Dec	Hx	Oct	Html	Chr
0	0	000	NUL	(null)	32	20	040	&#32;	Space	64	40	100	&#64;	@	96	60	140	&#96;	`
1	1	001	SOH	(start of heading)	33	21	041	&#33;	!	65	41	101	&#65;	A	97	61	141	&#97;	a
2	2	002	STX	(start of text)	34	22	042	"	"	66	42	102	&#66;	B	98	62	142	&#98;	b
3	3	003	ETX	(end of text)	35	23	043	&#35;	#	67	43	103	&#67;	C	99	63	143	&#99;	c
4	4	004	EOT	(end of transmission)	36	24	044	&#36;	$	68	44	104	&#68;	D	100	64	144	&#100;	d
5	5	005	ENQ	(enquiry)	37	25	045	&#37;	%	69	45	105	&#69;	E	101	65	145	&#101;	e
6	6	006	ACK	(acknowledge)	38	26	046	&	&	70	46	106	&#70;	F	102	66	146	&#102;	f
7	7	007	BEL	(bell)	39	27	047	'	'	71	47	107	&#71;	G	103	67	147	&#103;	g
8	8	010	BS	(backspace)	40	28	050	&#40;	(	72	48	110	&#72;	H	104	68	150	&#104;	h
9	9	011	TAB	(horizontal tab)	41	29	051	&#41;	)	73	49	111	&#73;	I	105	69	151	&#105;	i
10	A	012	LF	(NL line feed, new line)	42	2A	052	&#42;	*	74	4A	112	&#74;	J	106	6A	152	&#106;	j
11	B	013	VT	(vertical tab)	43	2B	053	&#43;	+	75	4B	113	&#75;	K	107	6B	153	&#107;	k
12	C	014	FF	(NP form feed, new page)	44	2C	054	&#44;	,	76	4C	114	&#76;	L	108	6C	154	&#108;	l
13	D	015	CR	(carriage return)	45	2D	055	&#45;	-	77	4D	115	&#77;	M	109	6D	155	&#109;	m
14	E	016	SO	(shift out)	46	2E	056	&#46;	.	78	4E	116	&#78;	N	110	6E	156	&#110;	n
15	F	017	SI	(shift in)	47	2F	057	&#47;	/	79	4F	117	&#79;	O	111	6F	157	&#111;	o
16	10	020	DLE	(data link escape)	48	30	060	&#48;	0	80	50	120	&#80;	P	112	70	160	&#112;	p
17	11	021	DC1	(device control 1)	49	31	061	&#49;	1	81	51	121	&#81;	Q	113	71	161	&#113;	q
18	12	022	DC2	(device control 2)	50	32	062	&#50;	2	82	52	122	&#82;	R	114	72	162	&#114;	r
19	13	023	DC3	(device control 3)	51	33	063	&#51;	3	83	53	123	&#83;	S	115	73	163	&#115;	s
20	14	024	DC4	(device control 4)	52	34	064	&#52;	4	84	54	124	&#84;	T	116	74	164	&#116;	t
21	15	025	NAK	(negative acknowledge)	53	35	065	&#53;	5	85	55	125	&#85;	U	117	75	165	&#117;	u
22	16	026	SYN	(synchronous idle)	54	36	066	&#54;	6	86	56	126	&#86;	V	118	76	166	&#118;	v
23	17	027	ETB	(end of trans. block)	55	37	067	&#55;	7	87	57	127	&#87;	W	119	77	167	&#119;	w
24	18	030	CAN	(cancel)	56	38	070	&#56;	8	88	58	130	&#88;	X	120	78	170	&#120;	x
25	19	031	EM	(end of medium)	57	39	071	&#57;	9	89	59	131	&#89;	Y	121	79	171	&#121;	y
26	1A	032	SUB	(substitute)	58	3A	072	&#58;	:	90	5A	132	&#90;	Z	122	7A	172	&#122;	z
27	1B	033	ESC	(escape)	59	3B	073	&#59;	;	91	5B	133	&#91;	[	123	7B	173	&#123;	{
28	1C	034	FS	(file separator)	60	3C	074	&#60;	<	92	5C	134	&#92;	\	124	7C	174	&#124;		
29	1D	035	GS	(group separator)	61	3D	075	&#61;	=	93	5D	135	&#93;	]	125	7D	175	&#125;	}
30	1E	036	RS	(record separator)	62	3E	076	&#62;	>	94	5E	136	&#94;	^	126	7E	176	&#126;	~
31	1F	037	US	(unit separator)	63	3F	077	&#63;	?	95	5F	137	&#95;	_	127	7F	177	&#127;	DEL

Source: www.LookupTables.com

Introduction

- Goals of this Lecture
  - Review Process of mapping Values between Binary and Decimal
  - Understand Integer Representation and Operations on them
  - Understand two schemes of representing Real Numbers
  - Understand Operations on Binary Representations of Floating Numbers

Integer Representation

- Overview of Integer Representation
  - Same to Process of Mapping Decimal Value into Binary Value
  - Unsigned Integer for representing Zero and Positive Integer
  - Signed Integer for representing both Negative and Positive Integer
  - Decimal Code for represent each digits (0 ~ 9) with four bits

Integer Representation

Unsigned integer

- Represented as binary number
- 8-bits Unsigned integer representation
    - 0   as 0000 0000
    - 1   as 0000 0001
    - ...
    - 254   as 1111 1110
    - 255   as 1111 1111

Integer Representation

- Signed Integer

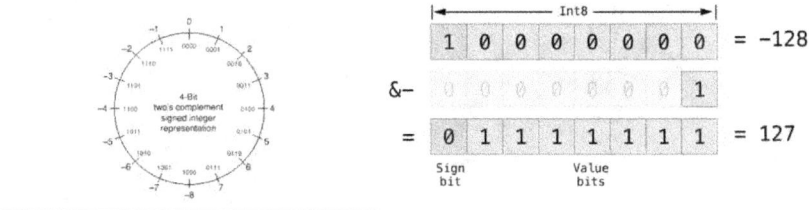

Figure 5-4. Signed integer representation (4-bit, two's complement)

Integer Representation

- Range

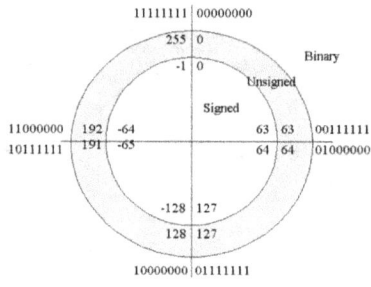
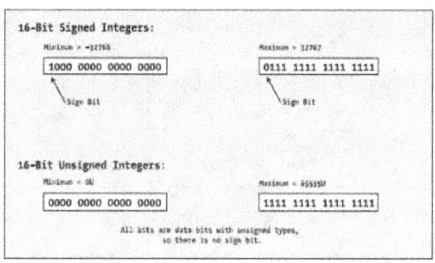

Integer Representation

- Decimal Code

Decimal	BCD	Gray
0	0 0 0 0	0 0 0 0
1	0 0 0 1	0 0 0 1
2	0 0 1 0	0 0 1 1
3	0 0 1 1	0 0 1 0
4	0 1 0 0	0 1 1 0
5	0 1 0 1	0 1 1 1
6	0 1 1 0	0 1 0 1
7	0 1 1 1	0 1 0 0
8	1 0 0 0	1 1 0 0
9	1 0 0 1	1 1 0 1

Operations on Integers

- Overview of Arithmetic Operations
  - Scheme of implementing Arithmetic Operations on Binary Representations of Integers
  - Implement Subtraction by adding 2's Complement
  - Use Addition and Shift for implementing Multiplication and Division
  - Finite Range of Integer by Fixed Length → Overflow and Underflow

Operations on Integers

• Addition and Subtraction

```
0 0 0 0 0 0 0 0 0 0 0 0 0 0 0 0
  0000000001000000            64
  0000000000101010           +42
  0000000001101010           106

1 1 1 1 1 1 1 1 1 1 0 0 0 0 0 0
  0000000001000000            64
  1111111111010110           -42
  0000000000010110            22
```

```
0 0 0 0 0 0 0 0 0 0 0 0 0 0 0 0
  1111111111000000           -64
  0000000000101010           +42
  1111111111101010           -22

1 1 1 1 1 1 1 1 1 0 0 0 0 0 0 0
  1111111111000000           -64
  1111111111010110           -42
  1111111110010110          -106
```

43

Operations on Integers

• Multiplication

```
    1011    Multiplicand (11 dec)
  x 1101    Multiplier   (13 dec)
    1011    Partial products
    0000    Note: if multiplier bit is 1 copy
    1011    multiplicand (place value)
   1011     otherwise zero
 10001111   Product (143 dec)
Note: need double length result
```

    Unsigned Integer

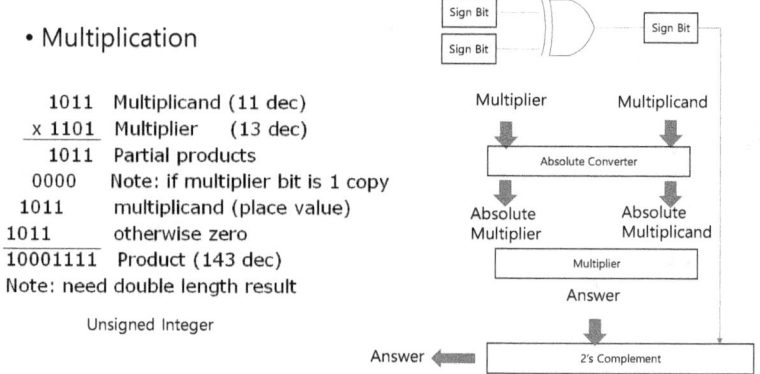

Operations on Integers

- Division

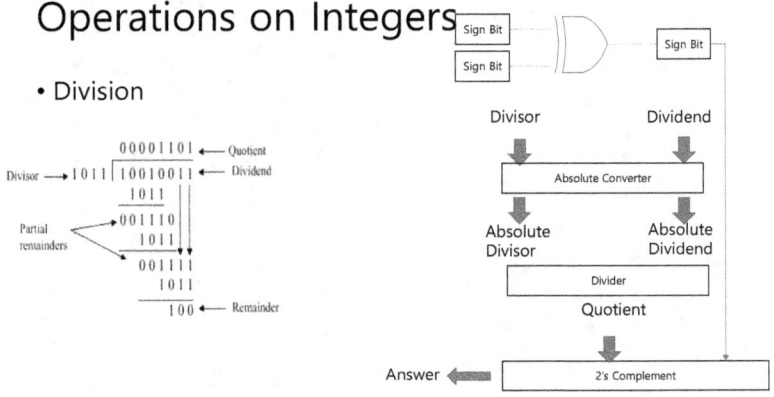

Operations on Integers

- Booth Algorithm

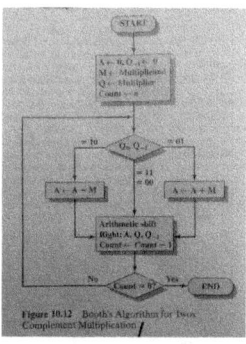

Figure 10.12 Booth's Algorithm for Twos Complement Multiplication

A	Q	Q_{-1}	M		
0000	0011	0	0111	Initial values	
1001	0011	0	0111	A ← A − M	First
1100	1001	1	0111	Shift	cycle
1110	0100	1	0111	Shift	Second cycle
0101	0100	1	0111	A ← A + M	Third
0010	1010	0	0111	Shift	cycle
0001	0101	0	0111	Shift	Fourth cycle

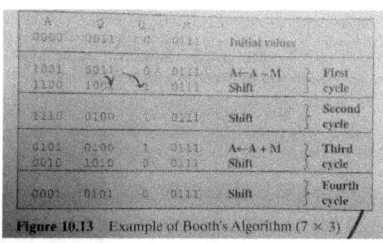

Figure 10.13 Example of Booth's Algorithm (7 × 3)

(a) (7) × (3) = (21)

(b) (7) × (−3) = (−21)

(c) (−7) × (3) = (−21)

(d) (−7) × (−3) = (21)

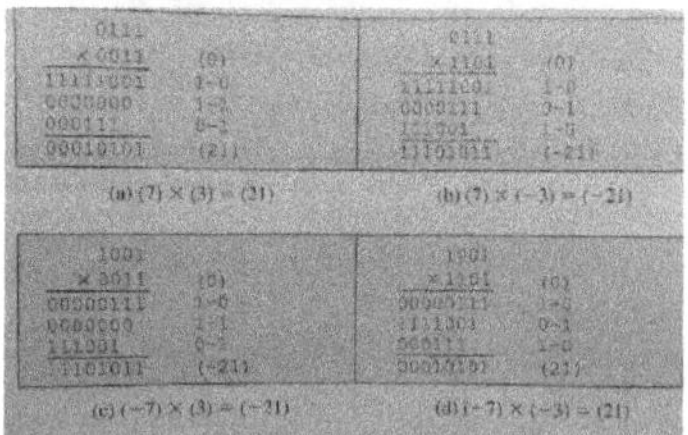

Figure 10.14 Examples Using Booth's Algorithm

Float Number Representation

- Overview of Float Number Representation
    - Represent Continuous Real Value into Binary Representation
    - Fixed Point Number: Sign bit + Integer Part + Fraction Part
    - Float Point Number: Sign bit + Significand + Exponent
    - IEEE Standard Format for representing Float Number: 16, 32, and 64 bits

Float Number Representation

• Fixed Point Representation

Integral Part	Fractional Part
8 bits	8 bits

Unsigned   0 ~ 255   Increment by 0.00390625
Signed   -128 ~ 127   Increment by 0.00390625

Integral Part	Fractional Part
K bits	L bits

Unsigned $0 \sim 2^K-1$ Increment by 2^{-L}
Signed $-2^{K-1} \sim 2^{K-1}-1$ Increment by 2^{-L}

Float Number Representation

- Float Point Representation

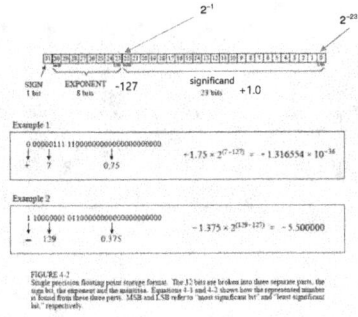

FIGURE 4-2
Single precision floating point storage format. The 32 bits are broken into three separate parts, the sign bit, the exponent and the mantissa. Equations 4-1 and 4-2 shown how the represented number is found from these three parts. MSB and LSB refer to "most significant bit" and "least significant bit," respectively.

Float Number Representation

- Range

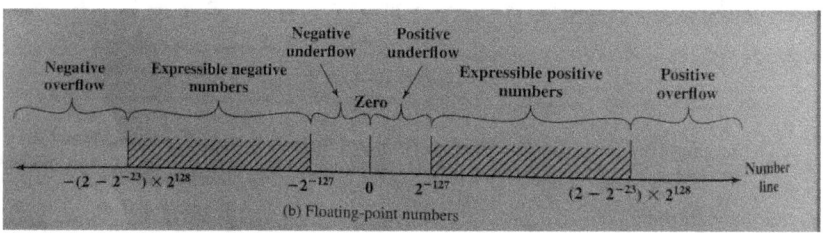
(b) Floating-point numbers

Float Number Representation
- IEEE Standard Formats

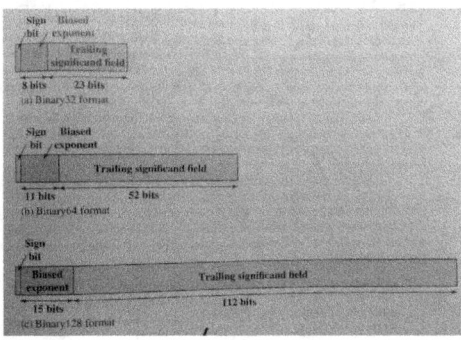

Operations on Float Numbers

- Integer → Float Number in Arithmetic Operation
    - Scheme of implementing Arithmetic Operations on Binary Representations of Real Number
    - Consider Exponent in Advance when performing Addition or Subtraction
    - Multiplication: Significand → Multiplication, Exponent → Addition
    - Division: Significand → Division, Exponent → Subtraction

Operations on Float Numbers
• Addition and Subtraction

Figure 10.22 Floating-Point Addition and Subtraction ($Z \leftarrow X + Y$)

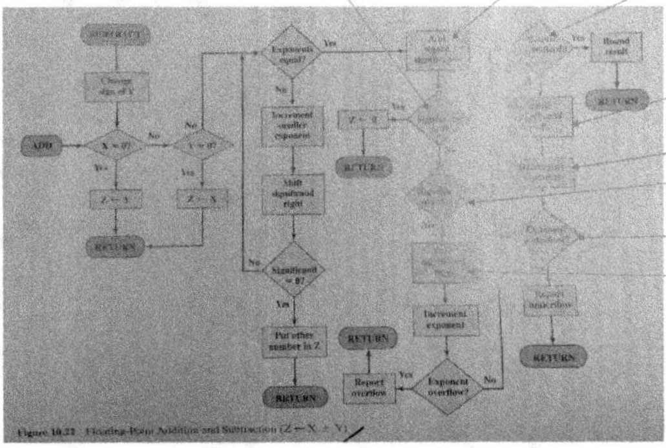

Operations on Float Numbers

- Multiplication

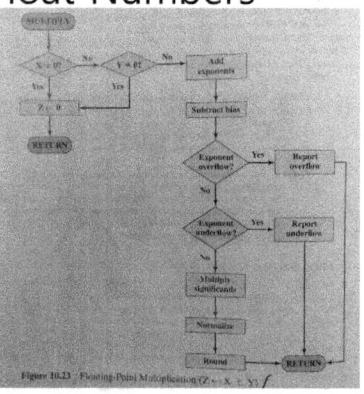

Operations on Float Numbers

• Division

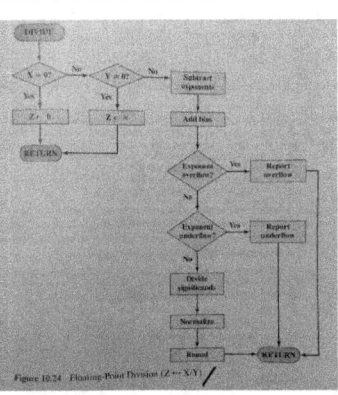

Figure 10.24 Floating-Point Division (Z ← X/Y)

Operations on Float Numbers

- Overflow and Underflow
    - Significand Overflow → Increment Exponent
    - Significand Underflow → Decrement Exponent
    - Exponent Overflow → Report Overflow
    - Exponent Underflow → Report Underflow

Digital Components
Lecture 03

Contents

- Introduction
- Decoder and MUX
- Adder
- Register
- Summary and Further Discussions

Introduction

- Digital Components for implementing ALU
    - Review Digital Circuits for studying Digital Components which are needed for implementing CPU and ALU
    - Four Components: Adder, Decoder, Multiplexer, and Register
    - Expand Components by attaching Smaller Sized Ones
    - Decoder for CPU and the others for ALU

Introduction

- Digital Logic Gates

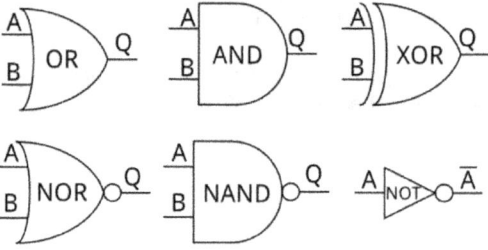

Introduction

- Digital Components

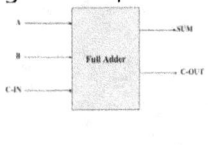

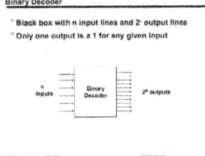

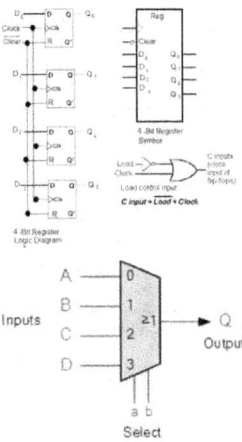

Introduction

- Combinational vs Sequential Logic Gates

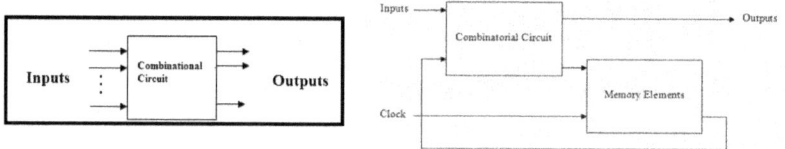

Introduction

- Goals of this Lecture
  - Review Logic Gates for understanding Implementation of Digital Components
  - Understand Decoder and MUX with respect to their Implementations and Expansions
  - Understand Adder with respect to its Function and Implementation and Obtain Skill of expanding it into its Larger Sizes
  - Understand Register which is implemented based on Synchronous Digital Circuit with respect to its Implementations and Expansions

Decoder and MUX

- Overview of Decoder & MUX
  - Decoder: Covert Binary Input into Bits where only one bit is 1
  - Use Decoder for generating Instruction Signal from Operation Code
  - MUX: Activating one among Multiple Lines
  - Use MUX for ..
    - Select Value from Register Files
    - Select Results from ALU

Decoder and MUX

• Function of Decoder & MUX

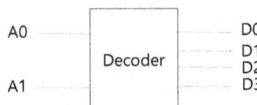

A1 A0	D3 D2 D1 D0
00	0001
01	0010
10	0100
11	1000

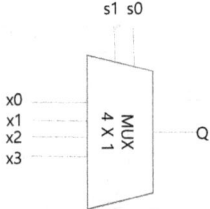

s1 s0	Q
00	x0
01	x1
10	x2
11	x3

Decoder and MUX

- Implementation of Decoder & MUX

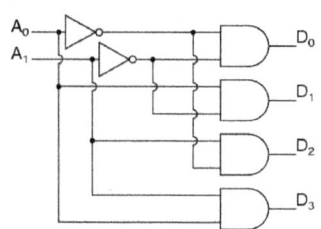
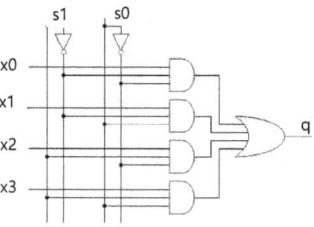

Decoder and MUX

- Expansion of Decoder and MUX

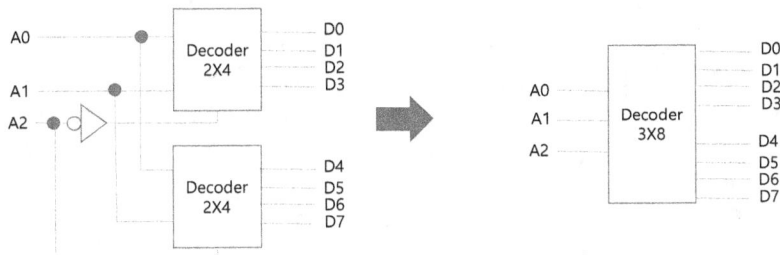

Decoder and MUX

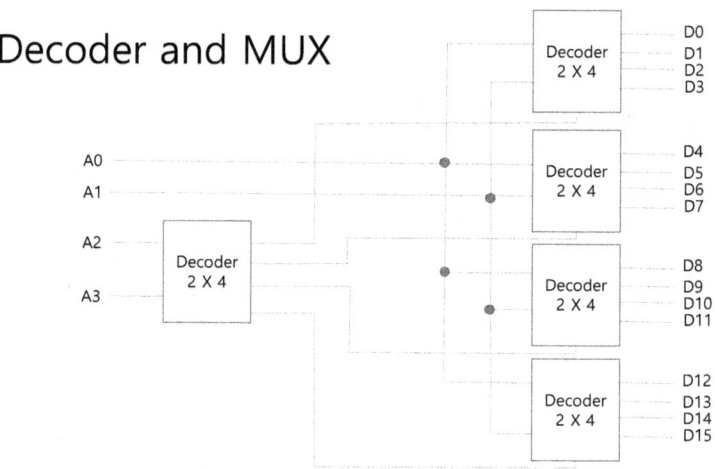

Decoder and MUX

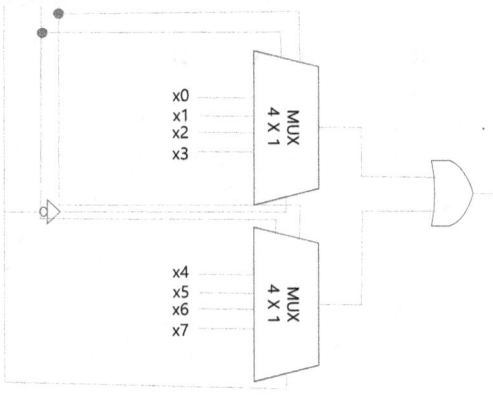

Decoder and MUX

- Decoder for CPU and MUX for ALU

Adder

- Overview of Adder
    - Combinatorial Circuit for adding Two Binary Values
    - Input: Two Binary Values, Output: Sum and Carry bit
    - Half Adder and Full Adder → 1 bit Adder
    - Implement n bit Adder by attaching 1 bit Adders

Adder

• Half & Full Adder

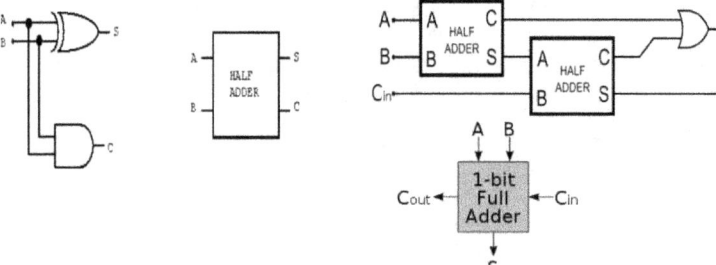

Adder

- 8 bit Adder

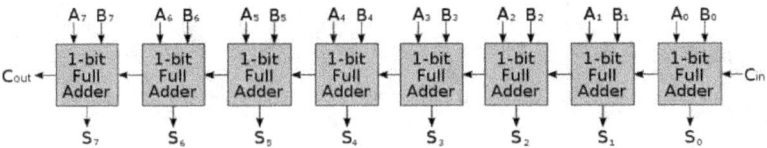

Adder

- Expansion into 32 bit Adder

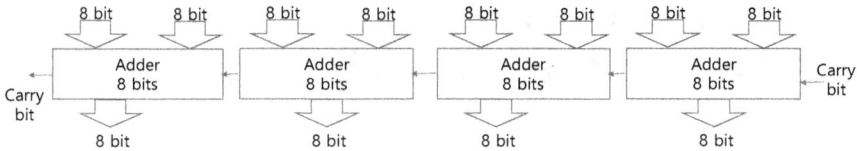

Adder

- Adder with Subtractor

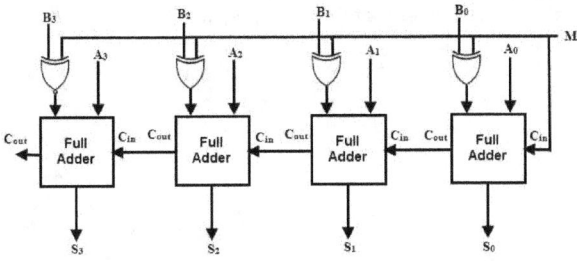

Register

- Overview of Register
    - Sequential Logic Circuit for storing Bit Values
    - Use D Flip Flop for implementing 1 bit Register
    - Implement n bit Register by attaching 1 bit Registers
    - Implement Register File or Memory by connecting Registers with Decoder

Register

- D Latch and D Flip Flop

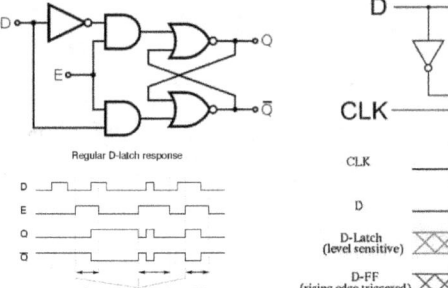

Register
- D Flip Flop for implementing Register

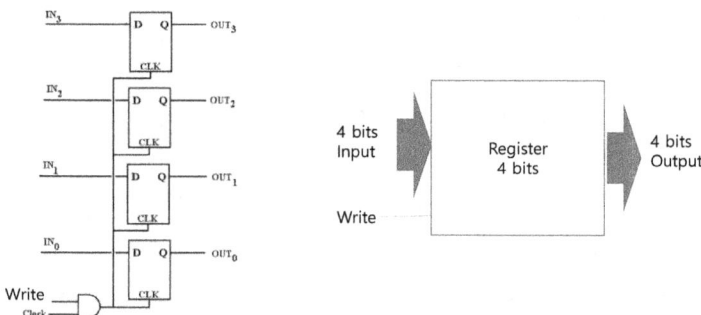

Register
- 16 bit Register

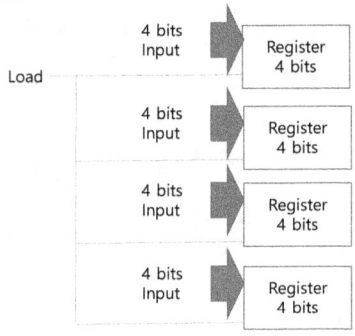

Register
• Register File

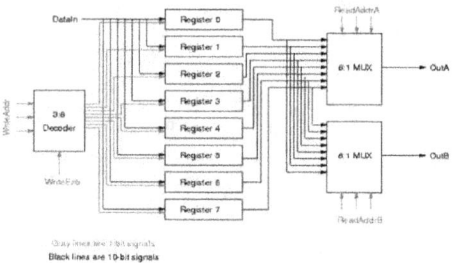

Summary and Further Discussions

- Summary
    - Logic Gates: AND, OR, XOR, and Inverter
    - Decoder and MUX
        - Decoder: Operation Code → Instruction Signal
        - MUX: Select One among Several Ones
    - Adder for implementing Arithmetic Operations in ALU
    - D Flip Flop → 1 bit Register → n bit Register → Register File

Summary and Further Discussions
• Decoder for Instruction Signal

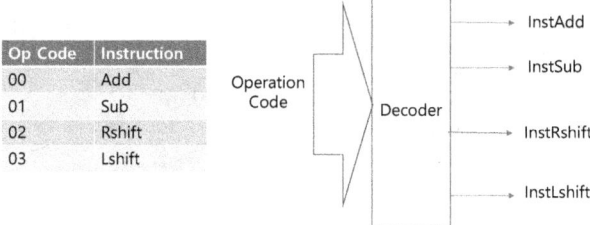

Op Code	Instruction
00	Add
01	Sub
02	Rshift
03	Lshift

Summary and Further Discussions

- MUX = Selector

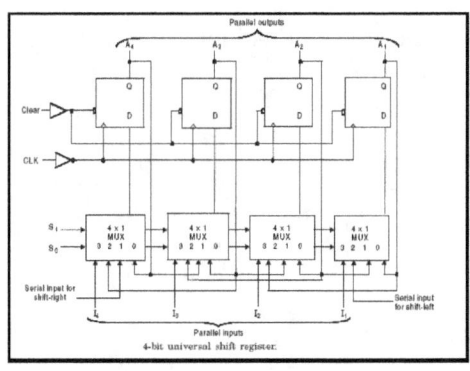

Summary and Further Discussions

- Two Registers and Adder

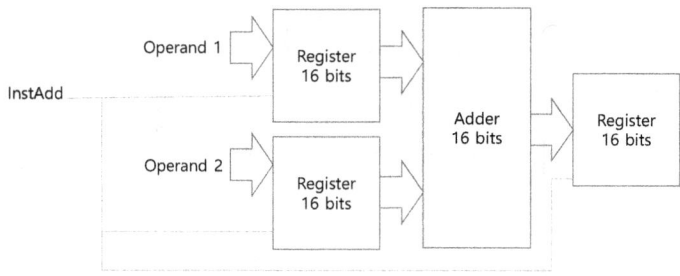

Summary and Further Discussions

- Operations with MUX

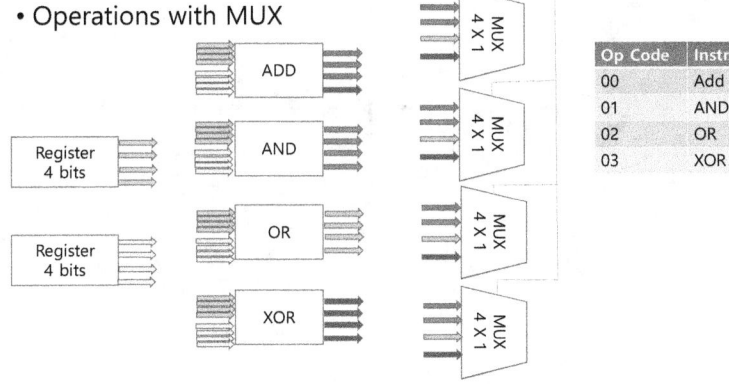

Op Code	Instruction
00	Add
01	AND
02	OR
03	XOR

Arithmetic Logic Unit
Lecture 04

Contents

- Introduction
- Adder with Subtractor
- Logic Operations
- ALU Structure
- Summary and Further Discussions

Introduction

- Overview of ALU Design
  - Implement ALU using Digital Components, Adder, MUX, and Registers
  - Assume Two Input Registers and One Output Register
  - Select One among Results computed by ALU through MUX
  - Connect ALU with CPU through Operation Code

Introduction

- Involved Components

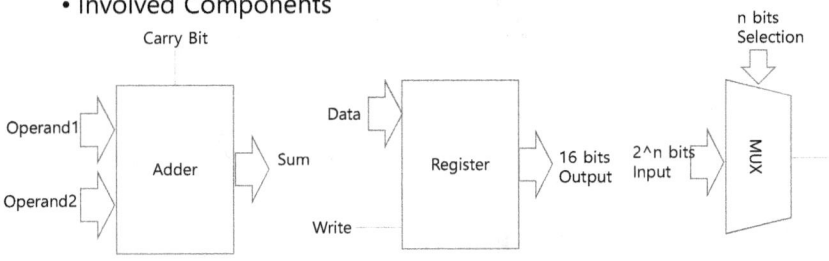

Introduction
• Frame of ALU Design

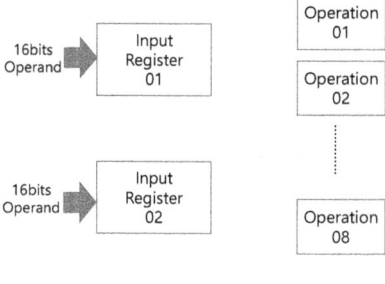
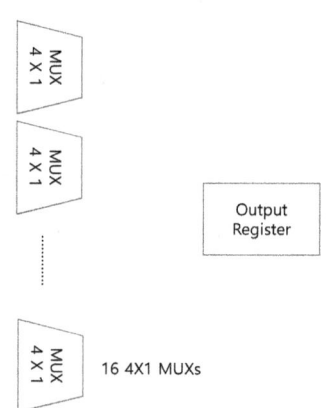

16 4X1 MUXs

Introduction

- ALU Operations

Operation Code	Operation
000	Input 1
001	Input 2
010	Neg Input 1
011	Add
100	Sub
101	AND
110	OR
111	XOR

Introduction

- Goals of this Lecture
    - Review Digital Components and Present Outline of ALU Design
    - Design Adder coupled with Subtractor
    - Design Logic, Shift, and Conditional Operators in ALU
    - Integrate Adder with ALU Components for making Entire Design

Adder with Subtractor

- Overview of Adder + Subtractor
    - Digital Component for Two Operations: Addition and Subtraction
    - Input: Two Binary Values, Carry Bit, and Subtract Bit
    - Output
        - Subtract Bit = 0: Sum and Carry Bit
        - Subtract Bit = 1: Subtracted and Carry Bit
    - Expansion from 4 bit to 16 bits

Adder with Subtractor

- Addition and Subtraction

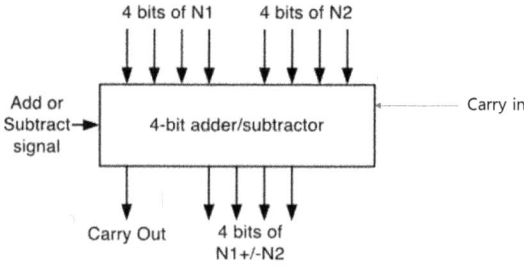

Adder with Subtractor

- Implementation

4-bit Binary Adder/Subtractor

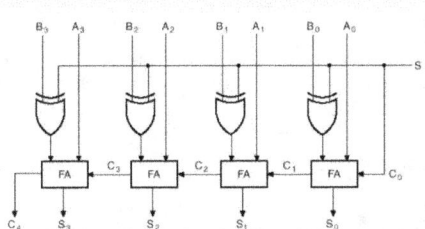

If S=0, performs A+B; if S=1, performs A-B
XOR gates act as programmable inverters

Adder with Subtractor

• Expansion

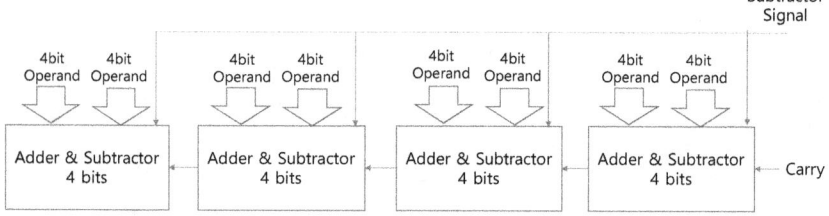

Adder with Subtractor

- Parallel Subtractor

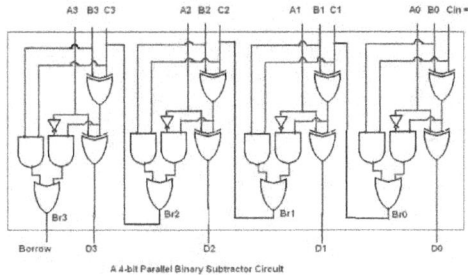

A 4-bit Parallel Binary Subtractor Circuit

Logic Operations

- Overview of Logical Operator
  - Unary Operation: Negation and Increment
  - Logic Operation: AND, OR, and XOR
  - Shift Operation: Right Shift and Left Shift
  - Conditional Operation: Greater than and Equal

Logic Operations
• AND and OR

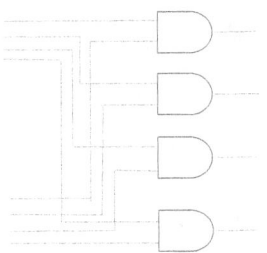 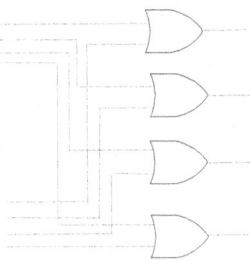

Logic Operations

- Shift Operation

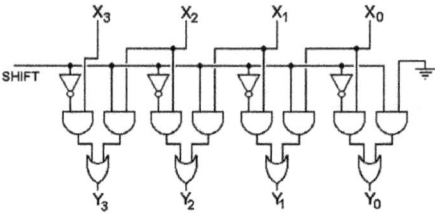

Logic Operations

• Conditional Operation

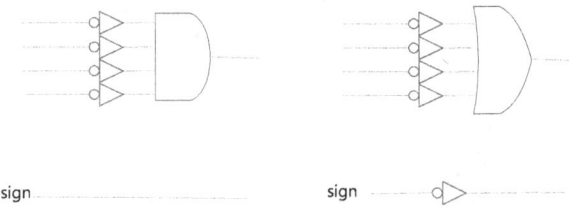

sign _____   sign _____▷○_____

Logic Operations

- Absolute Value

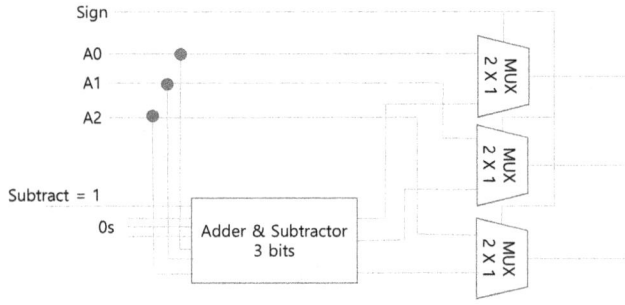

ALU Structure

- Design Specification
    - Two 4 Bit Input Registers and One 4 bit Output Registers
    - Additional Bits: Overflow Bit, Underflow Bit, and Conditional Bit
    - Perform All Operations at Same Time
    - Select one among Results from doing Operations by Operation Code

ALU Structure

- Opcode in ALU

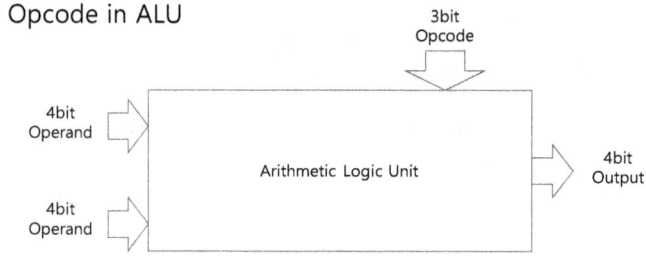

ALU Structure

- Components

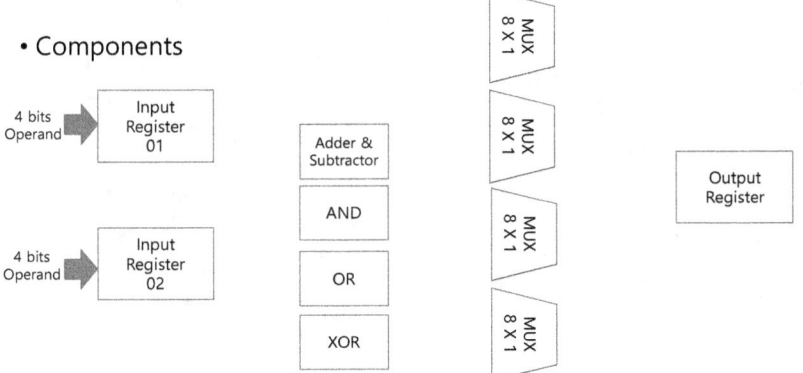

ALU Structure
• Implementation

Operation Code	Operation
000	Input 1
001	Input 2
010	Neg Input 1
011	Add
100	Sub
101	AND
110	OR
111	XOR

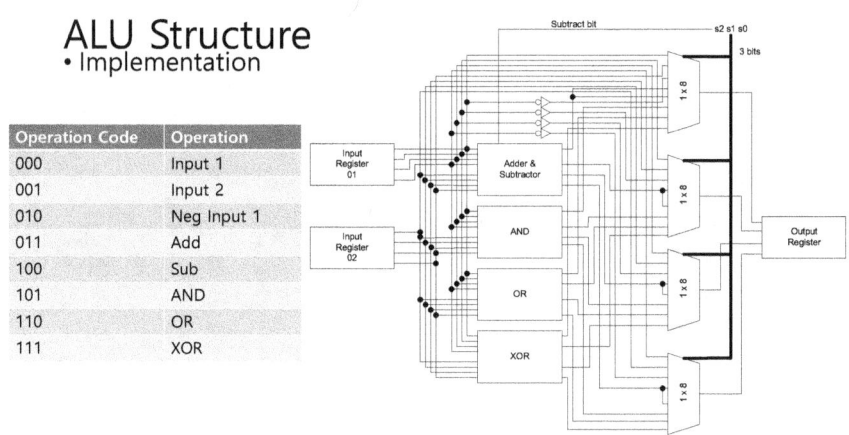

ALU Structure
• Instruction Signal

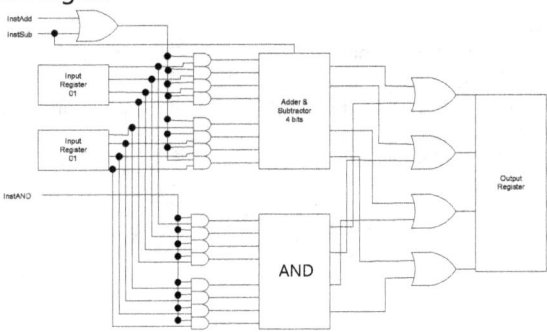

Summary and Further Discussions

- Summary
    - Components in designing ALU: Adder, MUX, and Registers
    - Digital Components: Addition + Subtraction
    - Implement other Operations: Logical, Shift, and Conditional Operations
    - Present Entire Design of ALU

Summary and Further Discussions
- BCD Code Adder

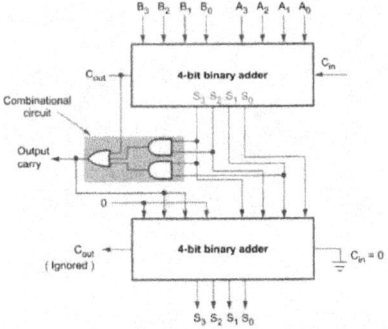

Summary and Further Discussions

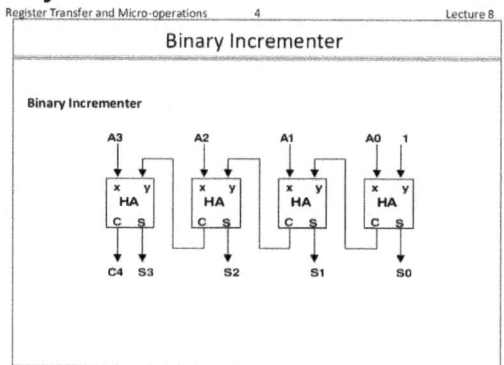

Summary and Further Discussions
- Register File in ALU

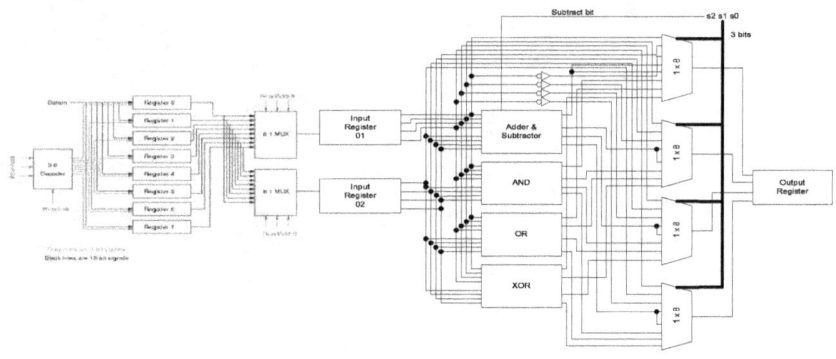

Summary and Further Discussions
- ALU Expansion

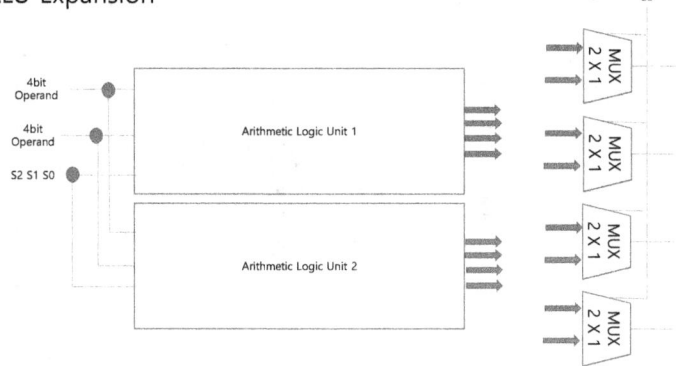

Instruction Set
Lecture 05

Contents

- Introduction
- Data Transfer Instruction
- Data Operation Instruction
- Control Transfer Instruction
- Summary and Further Discussions

Introduction

- Definition of Instruction
    - Single Operation Unit specified by Fixed Sized Bits
    - Instruction: Operation Code + Operands + Conditional Bits
    - Instruction → 64 bits
    - Use 16 bits for specifying Operations

Introduction

- Instruction List

Instruction Type	Instructions
Data Transfer Instruction	Load, Store, Move, Input, Ouput
Data Operation Instruction	Neg, Abs, Inc, Dec Add, Sub, Arshift, Alshift AND, OR, XOR, Lrshift, Llshift
Control Transfer Instruction	Jump, Skip, Call, Return EQZBranch, NEQZBranch, GTZBranch LTZBranch EQRBranch, NEQRBranch, GTRBranch LTRBranch

Introduction

• Instruction Format

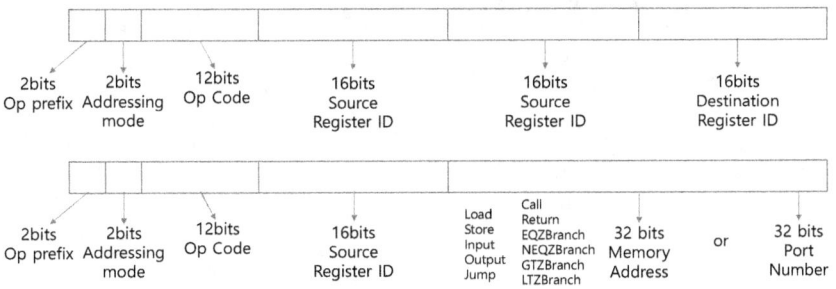

Introduction

- Instruction Code: Data Transfer Instruction

Op Prefix	Op Code	Instruction
00	0000 0000 0000	Move
00	0000 0000 0001	Load
00	0000 0000 0010	Store
00	0000 0000 0011	Input
00	0000 0000 0100	Output

Introduction

- Instruction Code: Data Operation Instruction

Op Prefix	Op Code	Instruction	Op Prefix	Op Code	Instruction
01	0000 0000 0000	Neg	01	0000 0000 0111	Alshift
01	0000 0000 0001	Abs	01	0000 0000 1000	AND
01	0000 0000 0010	Inc	01	0000 0000 1001	OR
01	0000 0000 0011	Dec	01	0000 0000 1010	XOR
01	0000 0000 0100	Add	01	0000 0000 1011	Lrshift
01	0000 0000 0101	Sub	01	0000 0000 1100	Llshift
01	0000 0000 0110	Arshift			

Introduction

Op Prefix	Op Code	Instruction
10	0000 0000 0000	Jump
10	0000 0000 0001	Skip
10	0000 0000 0010	Call
10	0000 0000 0011	Return
10	0000 0000 0100	EQZBranch
10	0000 0000 0101	NEQZBranch

Op Prefix	Op Code	Instruction
10	0000 0000 0111	GTZBranch
10	0000 0000 1000	LTZBranch
10	0000 0000 1001	EQRBranch
10	0000 0000 1010	NEQRBranch
10	0000 0000 1011	GTRBranch
10	0000 0000 1100	LTRBranch

Introduction

- Goals of this Lecture
  - Define Instruction Sets, Formats, and Binary Codes
  - Understand Functionally Data Transfer, Data Operation, and Control Transfer Instructions
  - Obtain Mapping Skill between Binary Machine Code and Assembly Code of Instructions
  - Obtain Instruction Programming Skill to given Problem

Data Transfer Instruction

- Overview of Data Transfer
    - Transfer Data between Registers and between Register and Memory
    - Assume No Cache Memory between Register and Memory
    - No Separation of Memory into Instruction and Data Memory
    - Transfer Data between Register and I/O Devices through Port Number

Data Transfer Instruction

• Transfer between Registers

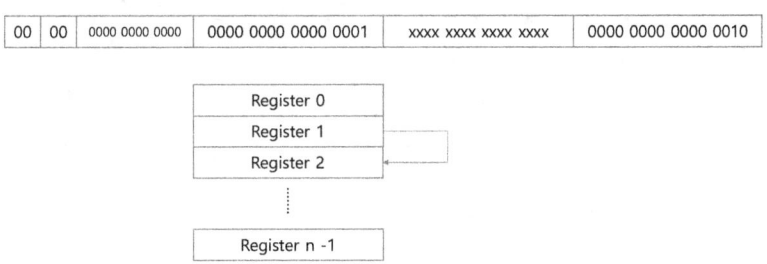

Data Transfer Instruction

• Load

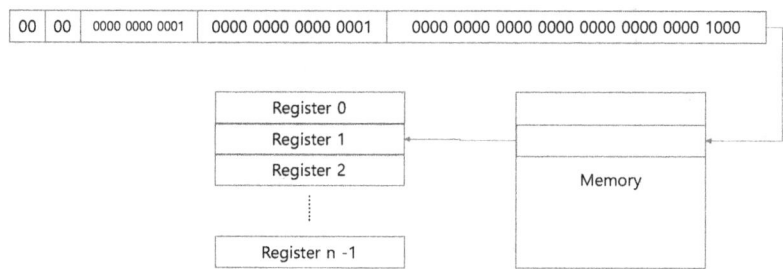

Data Transfer Instruction

• Store

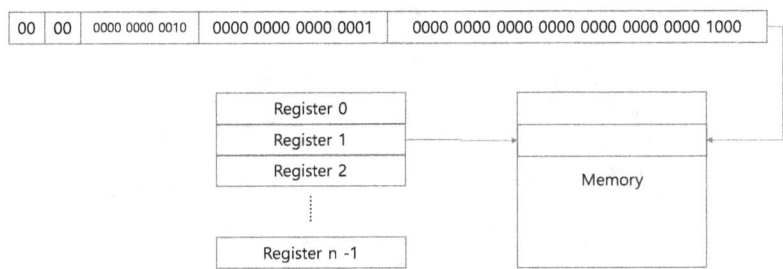

125

Data Transfer Instruction

• Input

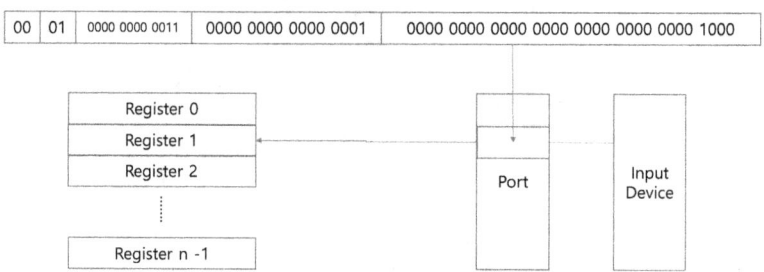

Data Operation Instruction

- Overview of Operations
    - Process Data by applying Operations
    - Involve Two Operands and One Result in performing Binary Operation
    - Indicate Operands by Register Mode
    - Data Registers → Register File accessed by Register ID

Data Operation Instruction

• Unary Operation: Neg, Abs, Inc, Dec

| 01 | 00 | 0000 0000 00xx | 0000 0000 0000 0001 | xxxx xxxx xxxx xxxx | 0000 0000 0000 0010 |

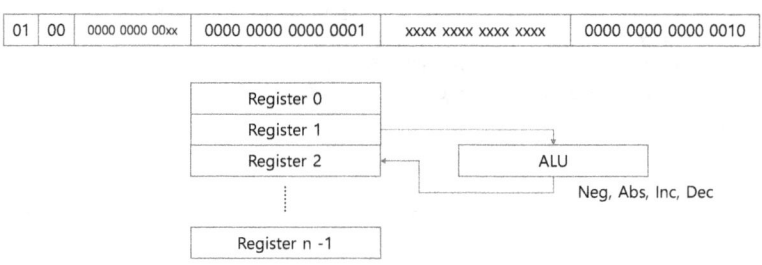

Data Operation Instruction
• Arithmetic Operations: Add, Sub, Arshift, Alshift

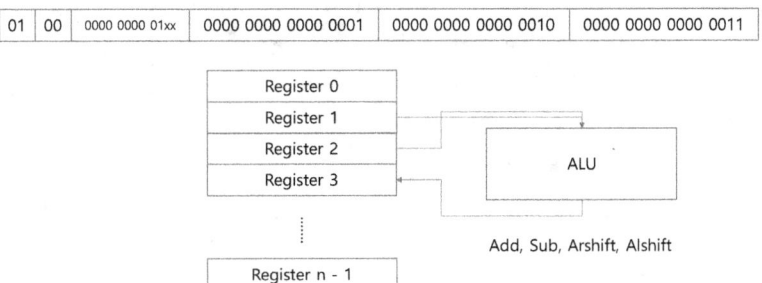

Data Operation Instruction
• Logic Operation: AND, OR, XOR, Lrshift, Llshift

01	00	0000 0000 10xx	0000 0000 0000 0001	0000 0000 0000 0010	0000 0000 0000 0011
01	00	0000 0000 1100	0000 0000 0000 0001	0000 0000 0000 0010	0000 0000 0000 0011

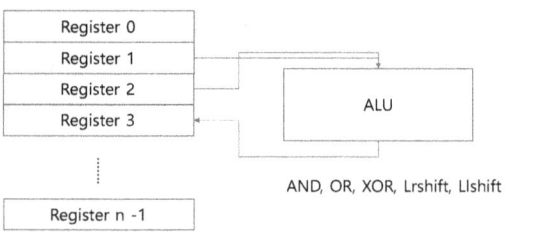

Register 0
Register 1
Register 2
Register 3
⋮
Register n -1

ALU

AND, OR, XOR, Lrshift, Llshift

Data Operation Instruction

• Shift Operation

```
        1101 0110 1100 1100                1101 0110 1100 1100
Arshift 0000 0000 0000 0001        Lrshift 0000 0000 0000 0001
   ➡   1010 1011 0110 0110           ➡    0110 1011 0110 0110


        1101 0110 1100 1100                1101 0110 1100 1100
Arshift 0000 0000 0000 0010        Lrshift 0000 0000 0000 0010
   ➡   1001 0101 1011 0011           ➡    0011 0101 1011 0011
```

Control Transfer Instruction

- Overview of Control Transfer
  - Instruction of jumping to Particular Address rather than Next Address
  - Instruction of selecting one among Branches depending on Condition
  - Jumping Instruction: Jump, Skip, Call, Return,
  - Branch Instruction: Equal, Nequal, Greater and Less

Control Transfer Instruction

• Jump and Skip

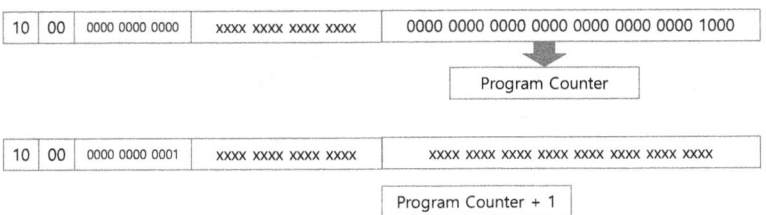

Control Transfer Instruction

• Procedure Call

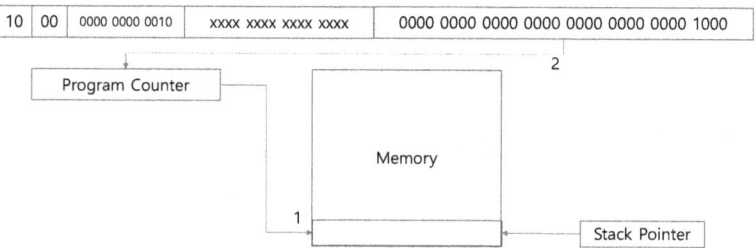

Control Transfer Instruction

- Return

| 10 | 00 | 0000 0000 0011 | xxxx xxxx xxxx xxxx | xxxx xxxx xxxx xxxx xxxx xxxx xxxx xxxx |

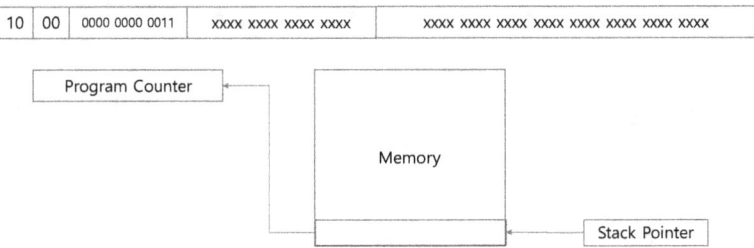

Control Transfer Instruction

• Zero Conditional Operations

| 10 | 00 | 0000 0000 0100 | 0000 0000 0000 0001 | 0000 0000 0000 0000 0000 0000 0000 1000 |

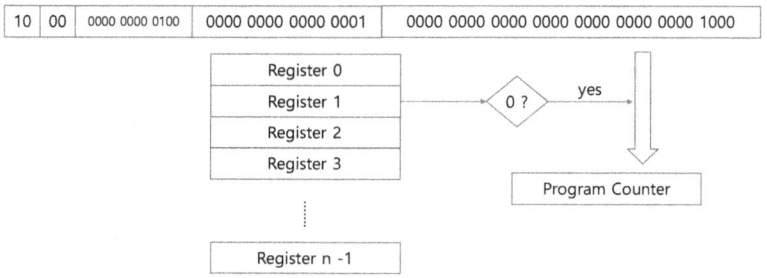

Control Transfer Instruction
• Value Conditional Operation

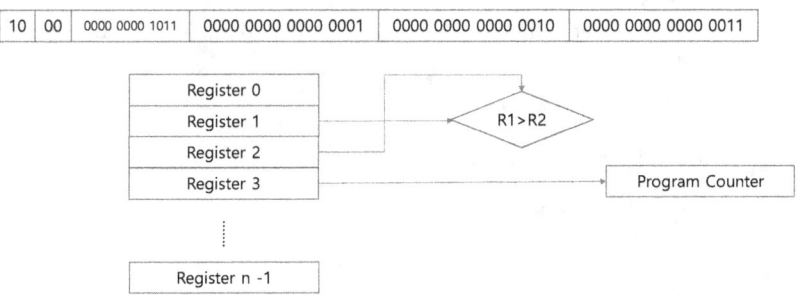

Summary and Further Discussions

- Summary
    - Define Instruction Set, Code, and Formats
    - Data Transfer Instructions: Mov, Load, Store, Input, and Ouput
    - Data Operation Instructions
        - Arithmetic Operations: Add, Sub, Neg, and Inc
        - Logic Operations: AND, OR, and XOR
        - Shift Operations: RShift and Lshift
    - Control Transfer Operation
        - Unconditional: Jump, Skip, Call, and Return,
        - Conditional: Equal, Nequal, Greater, Less

Summary and Further Discussions

- Hierarchical vs Flat Operation Code

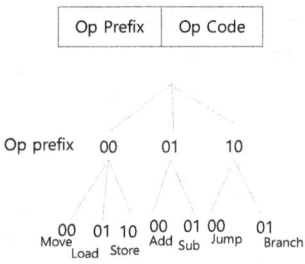

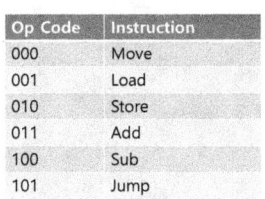

Op Code	Instruction
000	Move
001	Load
010	Store
011	Add
100	Sub
101	Jump
110	Branch

Summary and Further Discussions

• Input Device → Memory

00	01	0000 0000 0011	0000 0000 0000 0001	0000 0000 0000 0000 0000 0000 0000 1001
00	00	0000 0000 0010	0000 0000 0000 0001	0000 0000 0000 0000 0000 0000 0000 1000

Input R1 9
Store R1 8

                    Input Device (Port 9) → Register 1 → Memory 8

Summary and Further Discussions

• Memory → Output Device

00	00	0000 0000 0001	0000 0000 0000 0001	0000 0000 0000 0000 0000 0000 0000 1000
00	01	0000 0000 0100	0000 0000 0000 0001	0000 0000 0000 0000 0000 0000 0000 1010

Load R1 8
Output R1 10

Memory 8 → Register 1 → Output Device (Port 10)

Summary and Further Discussions

• Instruction Program

00	01	0000 0000 0011	0000 0000 0000 0001	0000 0000 0000 0000 0000 0000 0000 1001	
00	01	0000 0000 0011	0000 0000 0000 0010	0000 0000 0000 0000 0000 0000 0000 1001	
01	00	0000 0000 0100	0000 0000 0000 0001	0000 0000 0000 0010	0000 0000 0000 0011
00	01	0000 0000 0100	0000 0000 0000 0011	0000 0000 0000 0000 0000 0000 0000 1010	

Input R1 9
Input R2 9
Add R1 R2 R3
Output R3 10

Instruction Strategies
Lecture 06

Contents

- Introduction
- Addressing Modes
- Information Formats
- Procedure Call
- Summary and Further Discussions

Introduction

- Overview of Instruction Set Expansion
  - Alternative ways of defining Instruction Set, Formats, and Codes
  - Addressing Modes
    - Intermediate Mode
    - Direct and Indirect Register Mode
    - Direct and Indirect Addressing Mode
  - Survey Previous Cases of Instruction Formats
  - Procedure Call by Stack

Introduction

- Instruction with Zero, One, Two, Three Addresses

| Op Code | Register 1 | Register 2 | Register 3 |

R3 ← R1 Op R2

| Op Code | Register 1 | Register 2 |

R2 ← R1 Op R2

| Op Code | Register 1 |

AC ← R1 Op AC
AC: Accumulator

| Op Code |

AC ← Stack Op AC

Introduction

- Operand Indication

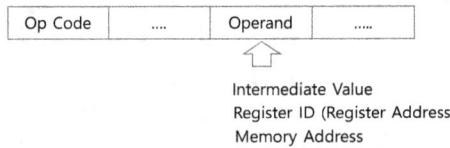

Intermediate Value
Register ID (Register Address)
Memory Address

Introduction

- Stack Operation for Procedure Call

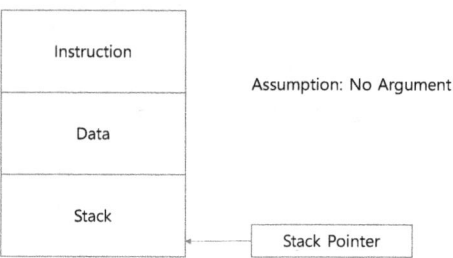

Assumption: No Argument

Introduction

- Goals of this Lecture
  - Consider Alternative Schemes of defining Instruction Set, Formats, and Codes
  - Understand Various Kinds of Addressing Modes
  - Explore Previous Cases of defining Instruction Formats
  - Understand Process of calling Procedure and Returning

Addressing Modes

- Overview of Addressing Mode
  - Scheme of indicating Operands
  - Intermediate Mode: Indicate Operands by Values
  - Register Mode: Indicate Operands by Registers
  - Addressing Mode: Indicate Operands by Memory Address

Addressing Modes

• Intermediate Mode

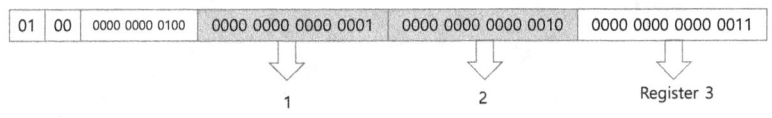

ADD 1 2 R3

Addressing Modes

- Direct vs Indirect Register Mode

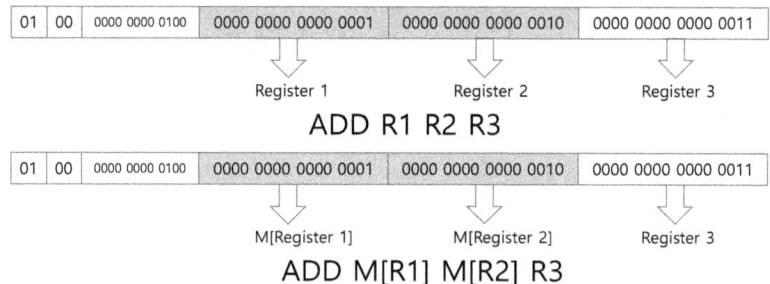

Addressing Modes

• Direct Addressing Mode

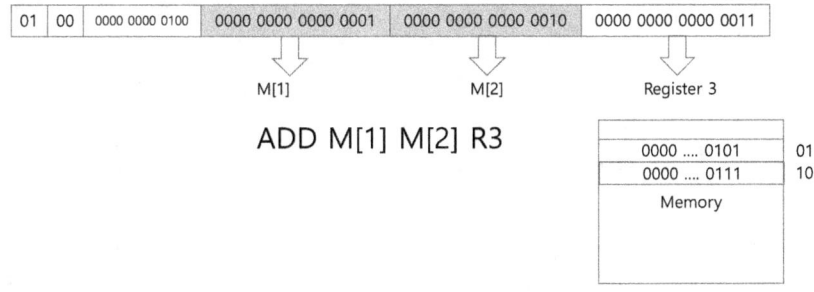

ADD M[1] M[2] R3

Addressing Modes
• Indirect Addressing Mode

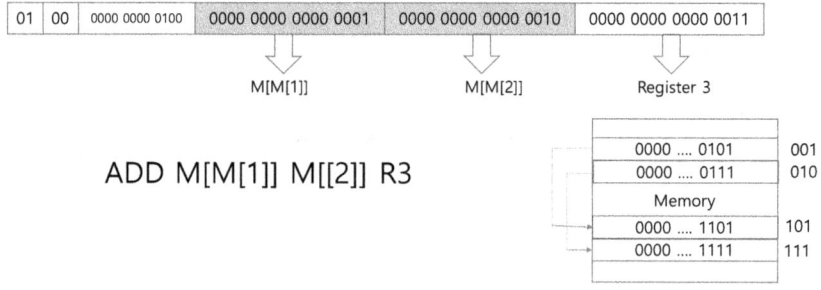

ADD M[M[1]] M[[2]] R3

Information Formats

- Overview of Instruction Formats
    - Instruction → Fixed Sized Bits
    - Various Schemes of partitioning Instruction into Operation Code and Operands
    - Define Addressing Modes as Strategy of indicating Operands
    - Define Instruction List and Conversion between Binary Code and Assembly Code

Information Formats

- IAS Computer

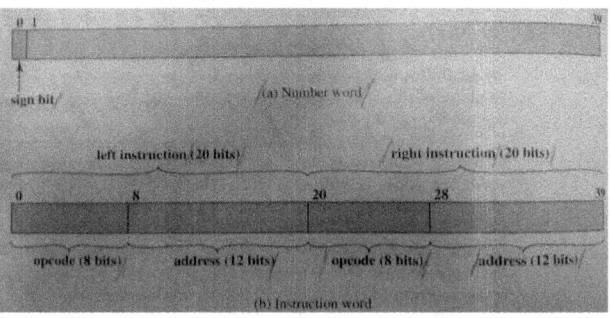

Information Formats

- MiniMips

Figure 5.4 MiniMIPS instructions come in only three formats: register (R), immediate (I), and jump (J).

R format:
| op (6 bits) Opcode | rs (5 bits) Source register 1 | rt (5 bits) Source register 2 | rd (5 bits) Destination register | sh (5 bits) Shift amount | fn (6 bits) Opcode extension |

I format:
| op (6 bits) Opcode | rs (5 bits) Source or base | rt (5 bits) Destination or data | operand/offset (16 bits) Immediate operand or address offset |

J format:
| op (6 bits) Opcode | jump target address (26 bits) Memory word address (byte address divided by 4) |

Information Formats

- PDP Family

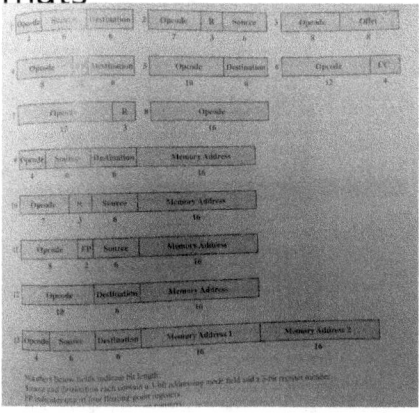

Information Formats

- ARM Instruction
- Acorn RISC Machine

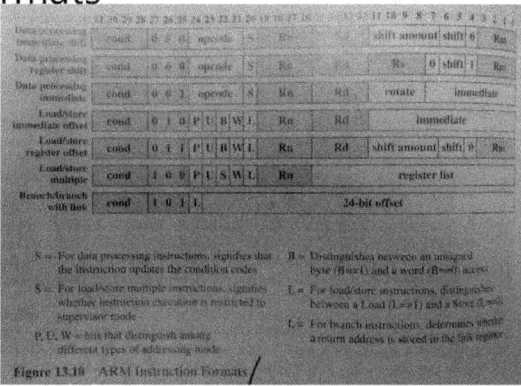

Figure 13.10 ARM Instruction Formats

Procedure Call

- Overview of Procedure Call
  - Fetch Instruction: Call Address
  - Store Address of Next Instruction (Program Counter) by pushing Stack
  - Execute Instructions in Procedure Body
  - Return to Main Program by popping Stack

Procedure Call

- Procedure Call and Return

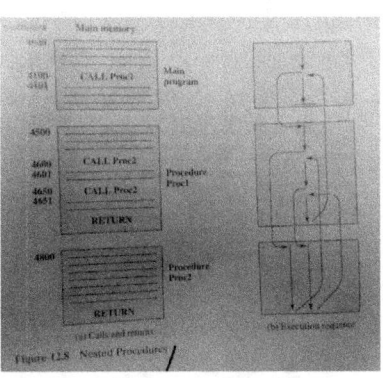

Procedure Call

- Procedure Call and Return with Stack

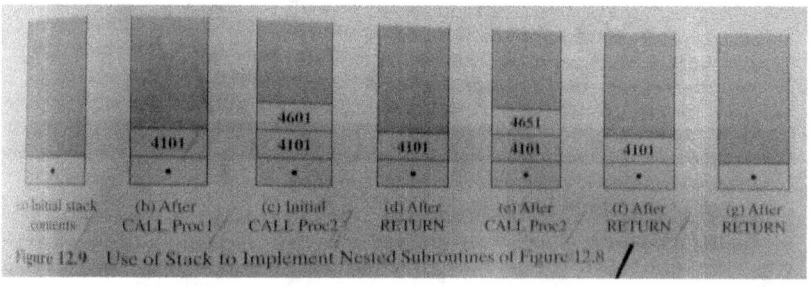

Figure 12.9 Use of Stack to Implement Nested Subroutines of Figure 12.8

Procedure Call
• Instruction Program

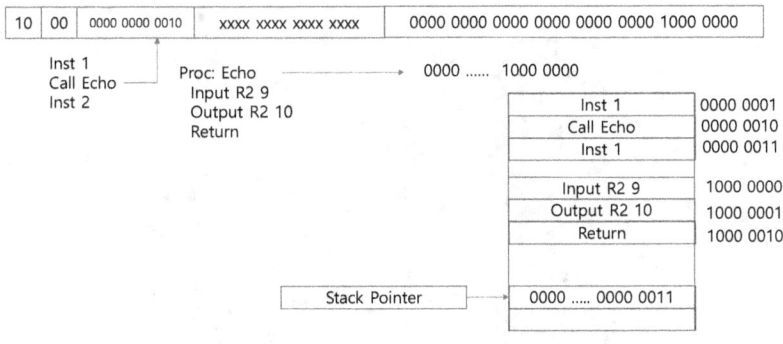

Procedure Call
• Considering Local Variables

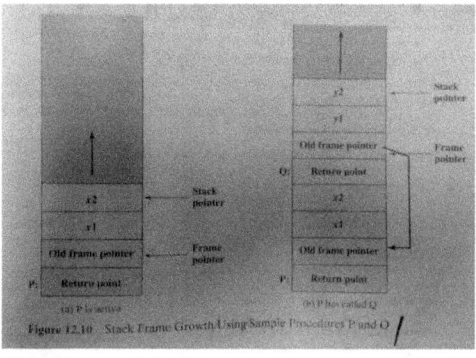

Figure 12.10 Stack Frame Growth Using Sample Procedures P and Q

Summary and Further Discussions

- Summary
  - Alternative Ways of defining Instruction Formats, Instruction Codes, and Addressing Modes
  - Addressing Modes: Schemes of indicating Operands
  - Survey Previous Instruction Formats
  - Two Instructions for Procedure Call: Call and Return

Summary and Further Discussions

- Additional Instructions

Op Prefix	Op Code	Instruction
00	0000 0000 0000	Move
00	0000 0000 0001	Load
00	0000 0000 0010	Store
00	0000 0000 0011	Input
00	0000 0000 0100	Output
00	0000 0000 0101	HAssign
00	0000 0000 0110	LAssign
00	0000 0000 0111	IndexLoad
00	0000 0000 1000	IndexStore

Summary and Further Discussions

• Higher and Lower Assignment

| 00 | 00 | 0000 0000 0101 | 0000 0000 0000 0001 | 0000 0000 0000 0000 0000 0000 0000 1000 |

Intermediate Mode

| Register 1 |

| 00 | 00 | 0000 0000 0110 | 0000 0000 0000 0001 | 0000 0000 0000 0000 0000 0000 0000 1000 |

Intermediate Mode

| Register 1 |

Summary and Further Discussions
- Index Load

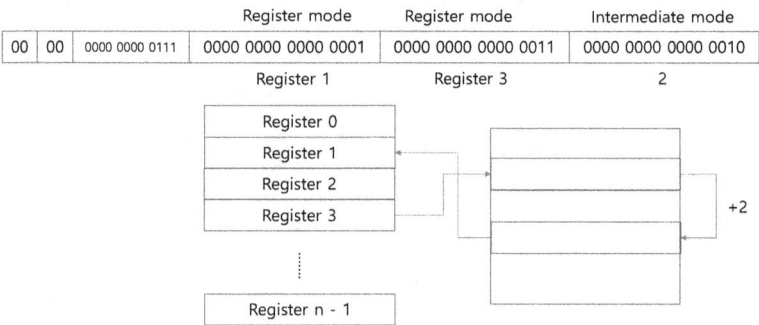

Summary and Further Discussions
• Index Save

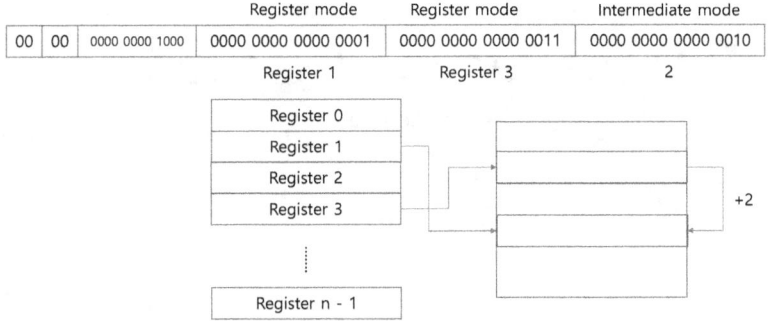

Instruction Execution

Lecture 07

Contents

- Introduction
- Data Operation Instruction
- Data Transfer Instruction
- Control Transfer Instruction
- Summary and Further Discussions

Introduction

- Definition of Instruction Execution
    - Process of executing Instruction with its own Cycle
    - Instruction Fetch: applicable to all Instructions
    - Instruction Specification ~ Finalization: Variable depending on Instruction
    - Execute Program by circulating Four Steps: Fetch ~ Finalization

Introduction

- Instruction Execution Cycle

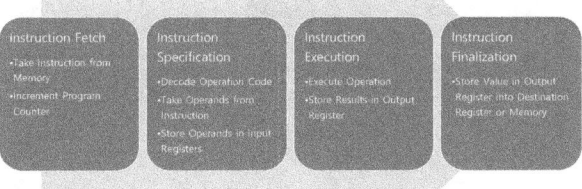

Introduction
- Computer Organization

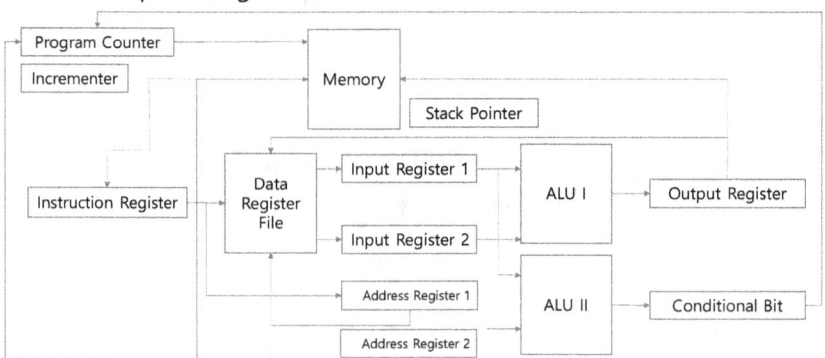

Introduction

- ALU II

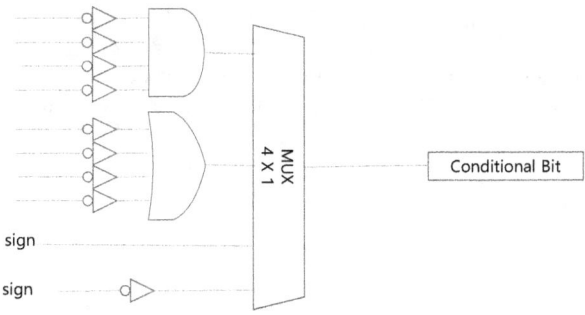

Introduction

- Goals of this Lecture
    - Review Four Steps of Instruction Execution Cycle
    - Understand Process of executing Data Operation Instructions
    - Understand Process of executing Data Transfer Instructions
    - Understand Process of executing Control Transfer Instructions

Data Operation Instruction

- Operations on Data
    - Instruction: Operation Code + Three Register IDs
    - Decode Operation Code and Store Values in Two Input Registers
    - Perform Operations on Values and Store Result in Output Register
    - Transfer Value of Output Register to Register in Register File

Data Operation Instruction

• Instruction Fetch

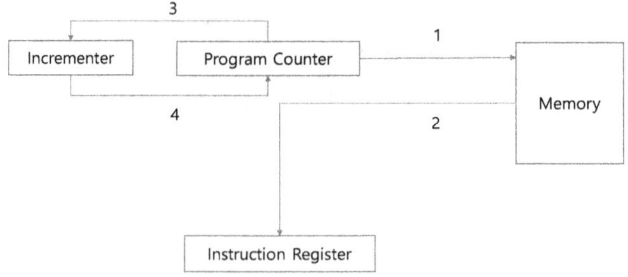

Data Operation Instruction

• Instruction Specification

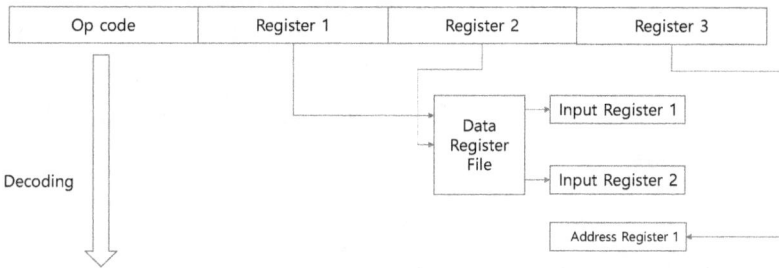

Data Operation Instruction
• Instruction Execution

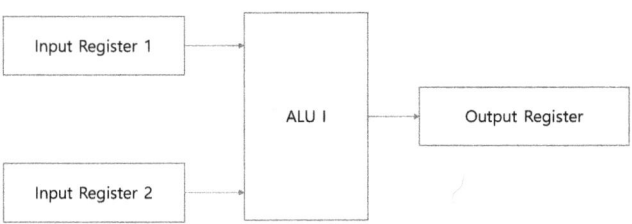

Data Operation Instruction

• Instruction Finalization

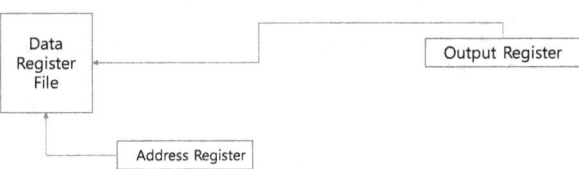

Data Transfer Instruction

- Overview of Data Transfer
    - Mov Instruction: Operation Code + Two Register IDs
    - Load and Store Instruction: Operation Mode + Register ID + Memory Address
    - Input and Output Instruction: Operation Mode + Register ID + Port Number
    - Need Conditional Bits for distinguishing memory and port number from each other

Data Transfer Instruction

• Instruction Specification: Move

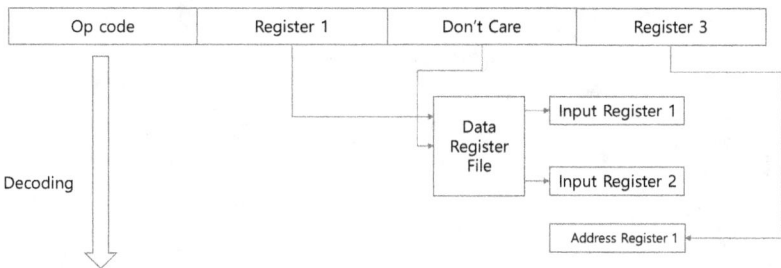

Data Transfer Instruction

- Instruction Execution & Finalization: Move

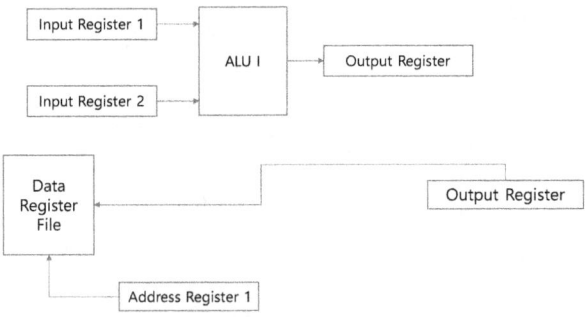

Data Transfer Instruction
• Instruction Specification: Load, Input

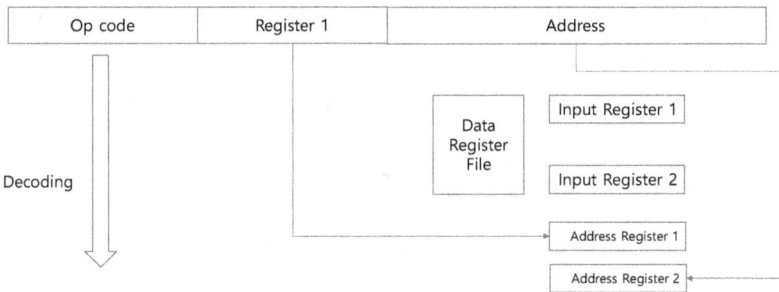

Data Transfer Instruction

- Instruction Execution: Load

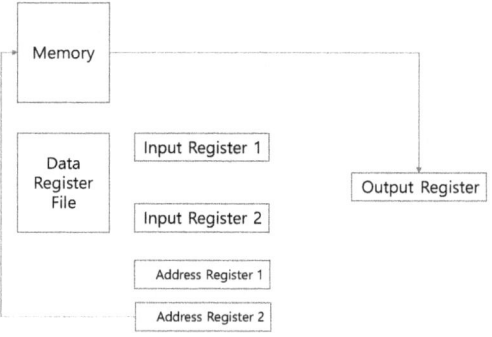

Data Transfer Instruction
• Instruction Execution: Input

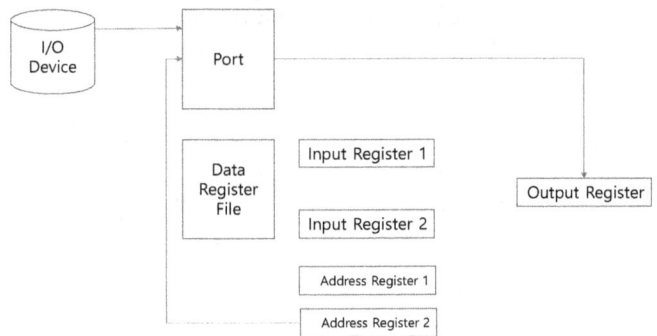

Data Transfer Instruction

• Instruction Finalization: Load and Input

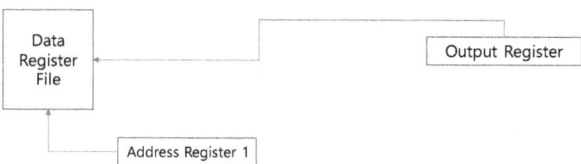

Data Transfer Instruction
• Instruction Specification: Store and Output

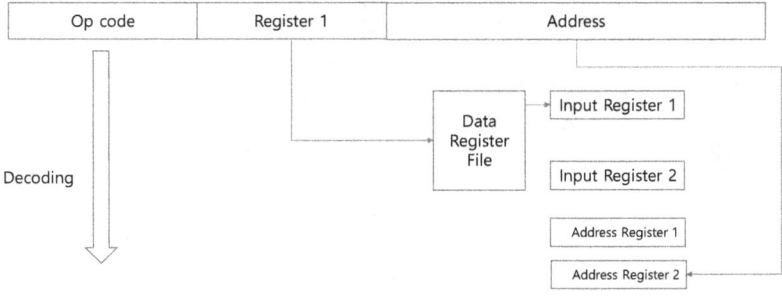

Data Transfer Instruction

• Instruction Execution: Store and Output

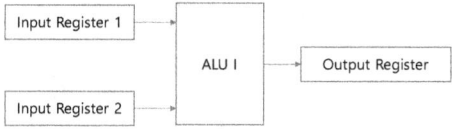

Data Transfer Instruction
• Instruction Finalization: Store

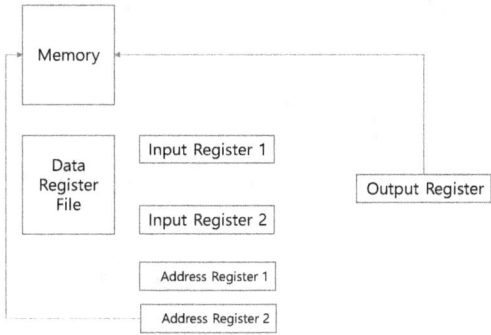

Data Transfer Instruction
• Instruction Finalization: Output

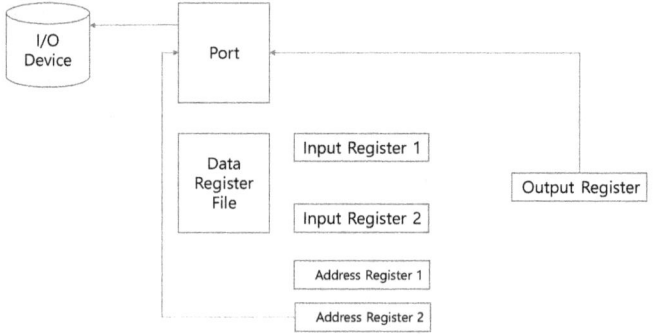

192

Control Transfer Instruction

- Overview of Control Transfer
  - Jump and Call Instruction: Operation Code + Memory Address
  - Return Instruction: Operation Code
  - Branch Instruction I: Operation Code + Register ID + Memory Address
  - Branch Instruction II: Operation Code + Three Register IDs

Control Transfer Instruction

• Instruction Specification: Jump, Call, Return

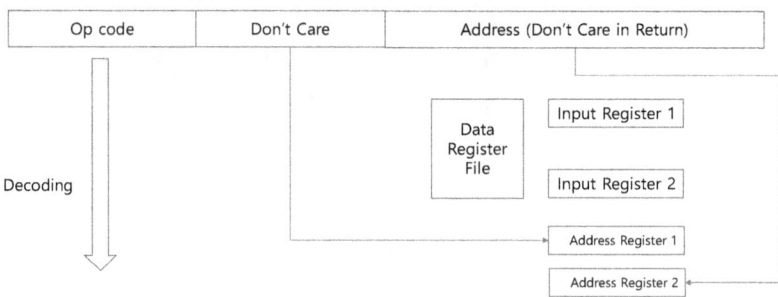

Control Transfer Instruction

• Instruction Execution: Call

Control Transfer Instruction

- Instruction Finalization: Jump, Call

Control Transfer Instruction

• Instruction Finalization: Return

Control Transfer Instruction

- Instruction Specification: EQZBranch, NEQZBranch, GTZBranch, LTZBranch

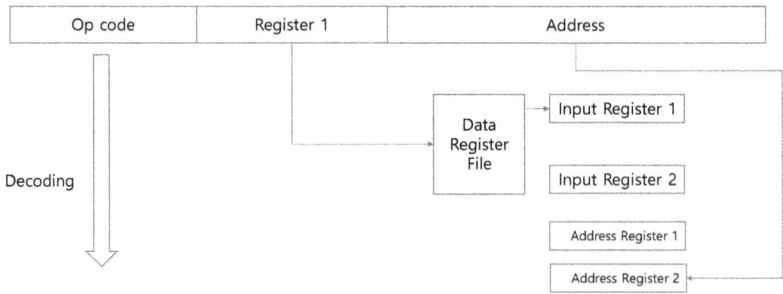

Control Transfer Instruction

- Instruction Execution: EQZBranch, NEQZBranch, GTZBranch, LTZBranch

Control Transfer Instruction

- Instruction Finalization: EQZBranch, NEQZBranch, GTZBranch, LTZBranch

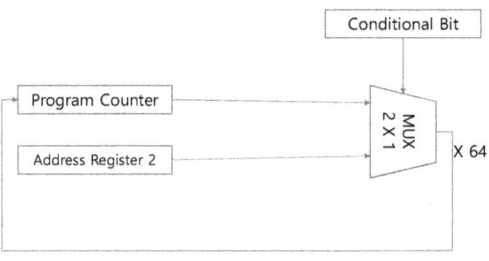

Summary and Further Discussions

- Summary
  - Instruction Fetch → Applicable to all Instructions
  - Instruction Specification
    - Decode Operation Code: All Instructions
    - Get two Input Values and Store into Two Input Registers: Data Operation
    - Get one Input Value and Memory Address: Store
    - Get Memory Address: Load, Jump and Call
    - Do Nothing: Return
  - Instruction Execution
    - Perform Operation on Input Registers and Store Result to Output Register → Data Operation and Branch Instruction
    - Read Data from Memory and Store it into Output Register → Load
    - Read Data from I/O Device and Store it into Output Register → Input
    - Input Register → Output Register: Jump, Save, Output
  - Instruction Finalization
    - Output Register → Register File: Data Operation, Load and Input
    - Output Register → Memory or I/O Device: Store and Output
    - Output Register → Program Counter: Control Transfer Instruction

Summary and Further Discussions

- Computer Instruction

Instruction Type	Instructions
Data Transfer Instruction	Load, Store, Move, Input, Ouput
Data Operation Instruction	Neg, Abs, Inc, Dec Add, Sub, Arshift, Alshift AND, OR, XOR, Lrshift, Llshift
Control Transfer Instruction	Jump, Skip, Call, Return EQZBranch, NEQZBranch, GTZBranch LTZBranch

Summary and Further Discussions

- Types of Instruction Specification

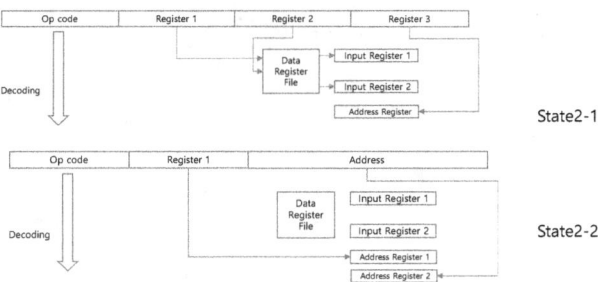

Summary and Further Discussions

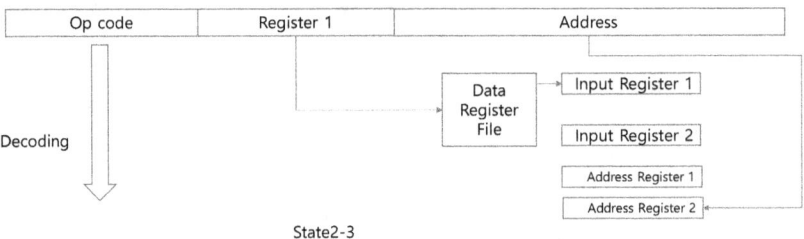

State2-3

Summary and Further Discussions

- Types of Instruction Execution

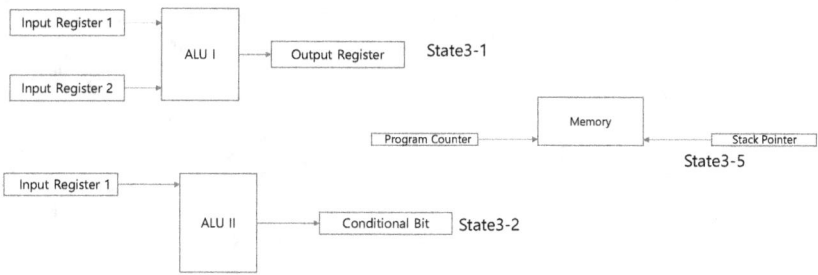

Summary and Further Discussions

- Types of Instruction Execution

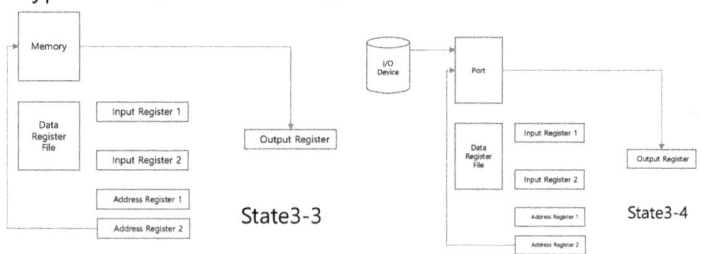

Summary and Further Discussions

- Types of Instruction Finalization

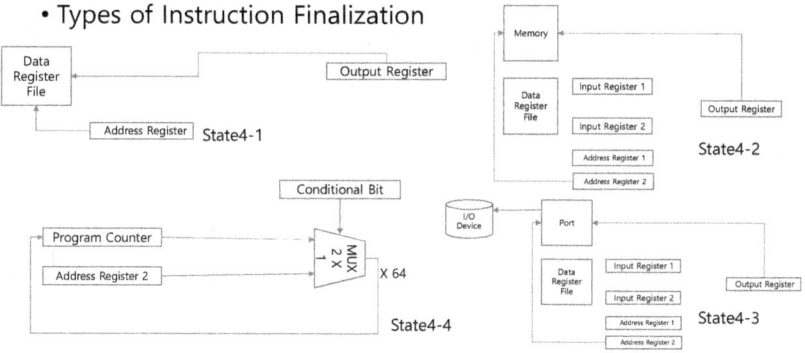

Summary and Further Discussions

- Type of Instruction Finalization

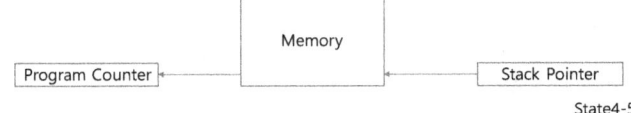

State4-5

Control Signal

Lecture 08

Contents

- Introduction
- Control States
- Control Signal Generation
- Micro-Programming
- Summary and Further Discussions

Introduction

- Definition of Control Signals
    - Signals for deciding Access Permission to Memory, Register File, and Registers
    - State Signals: States of Instruction Execution
        - Instruction Fetch: State 1
        - Instruction Specification ~ Finalization: State 2-1, ..., State 3-1,...., State 4-1, ...
    - Make List of Control Signals involved in executing Instruction
    - Express Boolean Expression of Instruction Signals and State Signals for each Control Signal

Introduction

- Instruction List

Instruction Type	Instructions
Data Transfer Instruction	Load, Store, Move, Input, Output
Data Operation Instruction	Neg, Abs, Inc, Dec Add, Sub, Arshift, Alshift AND, OR, XOR, Lrshift, Llshift
Control Transfer Instruction	Jump, Skip, Call, Return EQZBranch, NEQZBranch, GTZBranch LTZBranch

Introduction

- State Diagram

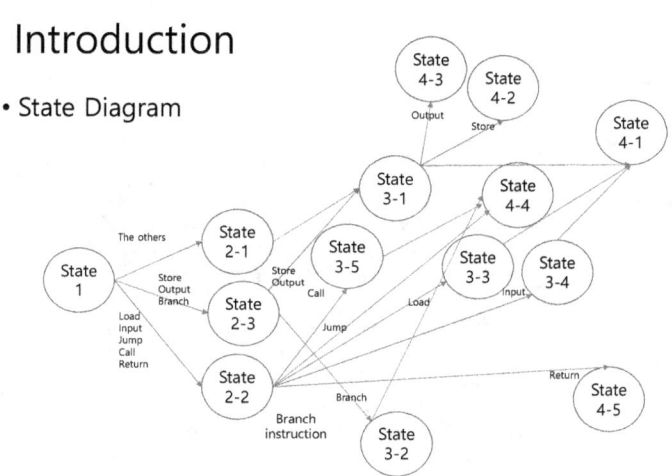

Introduction

- State Tracks of Instructions

Instructions	Track
Move, Data Operation Instructions	State 1 → State 2-1 → State 3-1 → State 4-1
Load	State 1 → State 2-2 → State 3-3 → State 4-1
Input	State 1 → State 2-2 → State 3-4 → State 4-1
Store	State 1 → State 2-3 → State 3-1 → State 4-2
Output	State 1 → State 2-3 → State 3-1 → State 4-3
Jump	State 1 → State 2-2 → State 4-4
Call	State 1 → State 2-2 → State 3-5 → State 4-4
Return	State 1 → State 2-2 → State 4-5
EQZBranch, NEQZBranch, GTZBranch, LTZBranch	State 1 → State 2-3 → State 3-2 → State 4-4

Introduction

- Goals of this Lecture
  - Make List of Control Signals and Instructions and Relations between them
  - Define States in each Step of Instruction Execution Cycle depending on Instruction Type
  - Design Circuit for generating Control Signals from Instruction and State Signals
  - Make Micro Instructions as alternative Scheme of generating Control Signals

Control States

- States of Instruction Execution Cycle
  - Instruction Fetch: State 1
  - Instruction Specification: State 2-1, State 2-2, State 2-3
  - Instruction Execution: State 3-1 ... State 3-5
  - Instruction Finalization: State 4-1, State 4-5

Control States
• Instruction Fetch: State 1

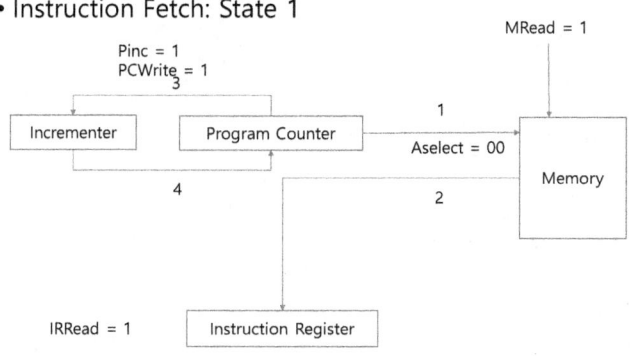

Control States

• Instruction Specification

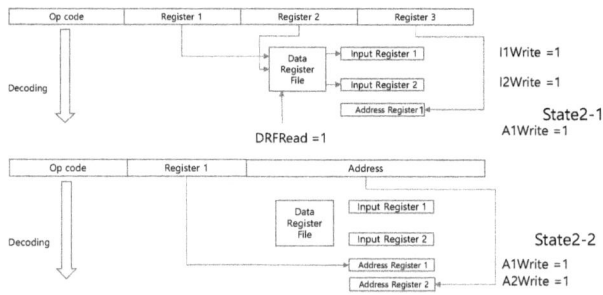

Control States

• Instruction Specification

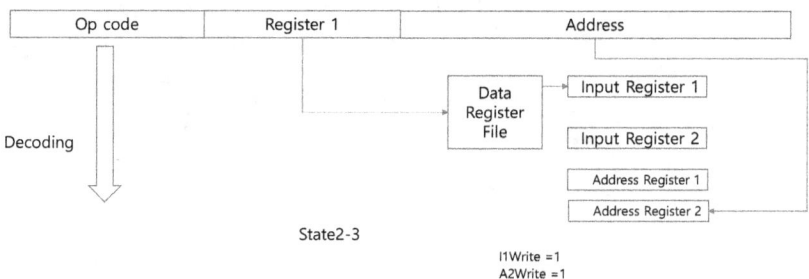

Control States

- Instruction Execution

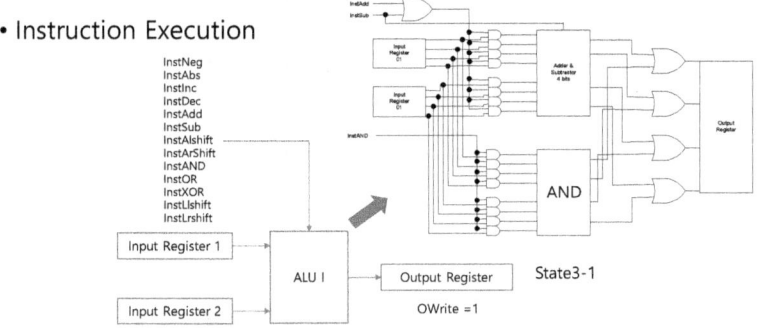

Control States

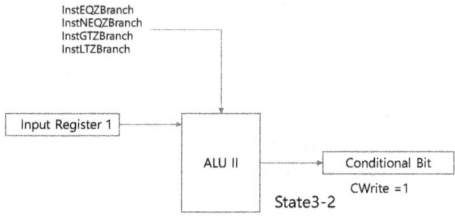

State3-2

Control States

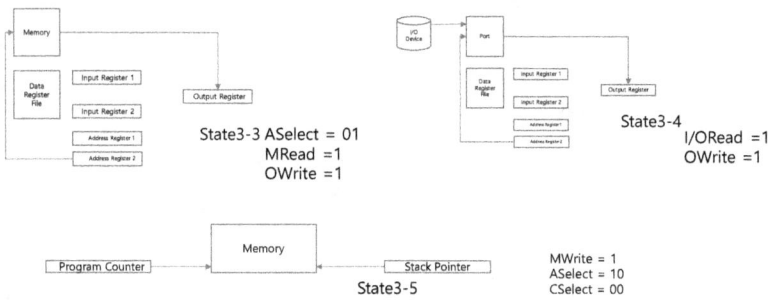

Control States

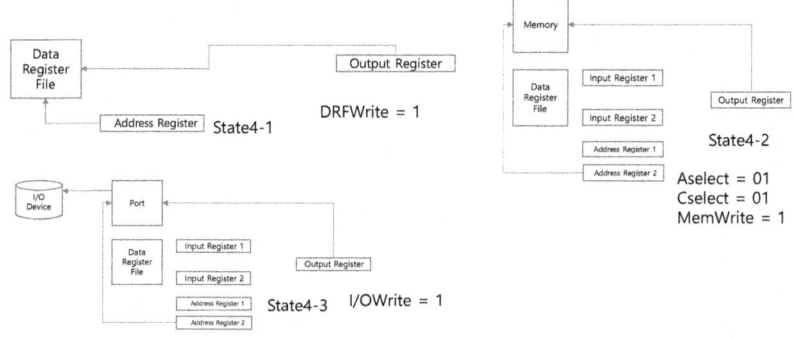

Control States

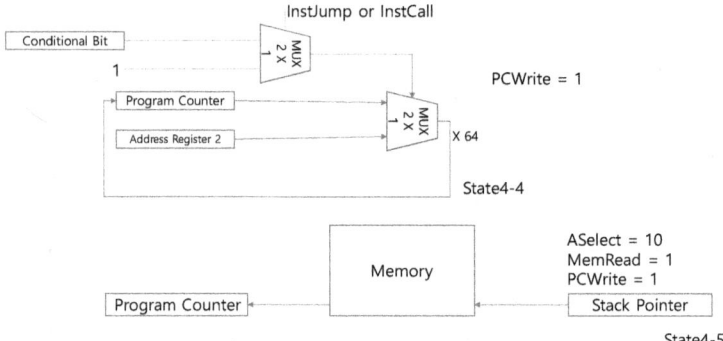

Control Signal Generation

- Overview of Control Signals
    - Operation Code → Single Instruction Signal by Decoder
    - Instruction Cycle + Instruction → Control State
    - Control State (Main) + Instruction → Control Signal
    - Design Circuit for generating Control Signals

Control Signal Generation

- Operation Code Decoding

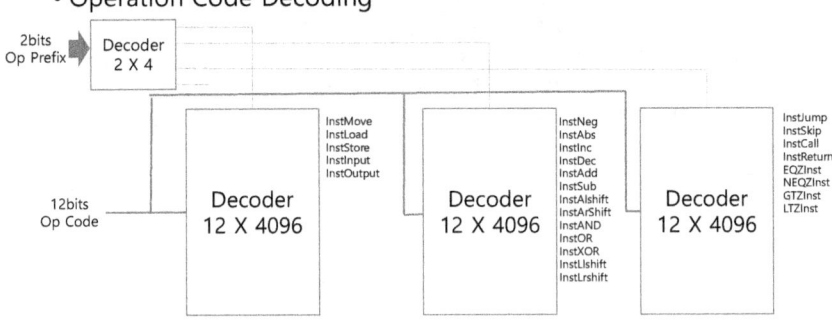

Control Signal Generation

	Clock 1	Clock 2	Clock 3	Clock 4
InstMove	ControlSt1	ControlSt2-1	ContorlSt3-1	ContorlSt4-1
InstLoad	ControlSt1	ControlSt2-2	ContorlSt3-3	ContorlSt4-1
InstInput	ControlSt1	ControlSt2-2	ContorlSt3-4	ContorlSt4-1
InstStore	ControlSt1	ControlSt2-3	ContorlSt3-1	ContorlSt4-2
InstOutput	ControlSt1	ControlSt2-3	ContorlSt3-1	ContorlSt4-3
InstDO	ControlSt1	ControlSt2-1	ContorlSt3-1	ContorlSt4-1
InstJump	ControlSt1	ControlSt2-2	Don't Care	ContorlSt4-4
InstCall	ControlSt1	ControlSt2-2	ContorlSt3-5	ContorlSt4-4
InstReturn	ControlSt1	ControlSt2-2	Don't Care	ContorlSt4-5
InstBR	ControlSt1	ControlSt2-3	ContorlSt3-2	ContorlSt4-4

InstBR = EQZInst V NEQZInst V GTZInst V LTZInst

InstDO = InstNeg V InstAbs V InstInc V InstDec V InstAdd V InstSub V InstAlshift V InstArShift V InstAND V InstOR V InstXOR V InstLlshift V InstLrshift

Control Signal Generation

	IRRead	PCWrite	PIoc	DRRead	DRWrite	IRWrite	MRead	MWrite	J1Write	T2Write	A1Write	A2Write	OWrite	CWrite	ASelect	CSelect	I/ORead	I/OWrite
State 1	1	1	1	0	0	1	1	0	0	0	0	0	0	0	00	xx	0	0
State 2-1	0	0	0	1	0	0	0	0	1	1	1	0	0	0	xx	xx	0	0
State 2-2	0	0	0	0	0	0	0	0	0	0	1	1	0	0	Xx	Xx	0	0
State 2-3	0	0	0	0	0	0	0	0	1	0	0	1	0	0	Xx	Xx	0	0
State 3-1	0	0	0	0	0	0	0	0	0	0	0	0	1	0	xx	xx	0	0
State 3-2	0	0	0	0	0	0	0	0	0	0	0	0	0	1	Xx	xx	0	0
State 3-3	0	0	0	0	0	0	1	0	0	0	0	0	1	0	01	Xx	0	0
State 3-4	0	0	0	0	0	0	0	0	0	0	0	0	1	0	Xx	Xx	1	0
State 3-5	0	0	0	0	0	0	0	1	0	0	0	0	0	0	10	00	0	0
State 4-1	0	0	0	0	1	0	0	0	0	0	0	0	0	0	xx	xx	0	0
State 4-2	0	0	0	0	0	0	0	1	0	0	0	0	0	0	01	01	0	0
State 4-3	0	0	0	0	0	0	0	0	0	0	0	0	0	0	xx	Xx	0	1
State 4-4	0	1	0	0	0	0	0	0	0	0	0	0	0	0	xx	xx	0	0
State 4-5	0	1	0	0	0	1	0	0	0	0	0	0	0	0	10	Xx	0	0

Control Signal Generation

- Boolean Expression

    PCWrite = ControlSt1 ∨ ControlSt4-4 ∨ ControlSt4-5
    Pinc = ControlSt1
    DRFRead = ControlSt2-1
    DRFWrite = ControlSt4-1
    ......

Micro-Programming

- Overview of Micro Programming
    - Instructions for generating Control Signals as alternative Way to Hardware Implementation
    - More Flexible but Slower Execution
    - Instruction ← RAM vs Micro Instruction ← ROM
    - Fetch Micro Instruction by Operation Code

Micro-Programming
- Micro Instruction Format

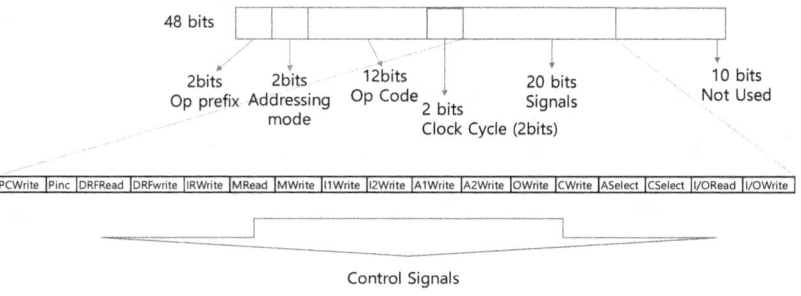

Micro-Programming

- Micro Instruction Fetch

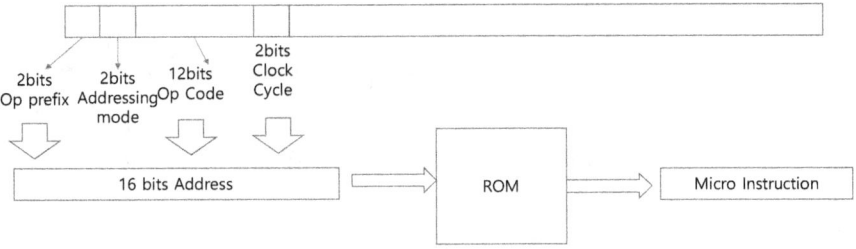

Micro-Programming
• Control Signal Generation

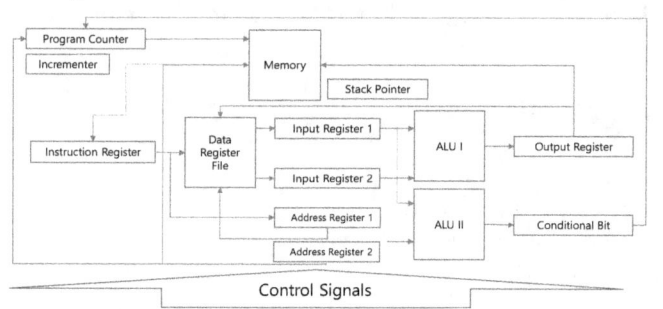

Micro-Programming

- Hardware Implementation vs Micro Programming

	Hardware Implementation	Micro Programming
Instruction Expansion	Difficult	Easy
Speed	Fast	Slow
Design Modification	Difficult	Easy
Location	Inside CPU	ROM

Summary and Further Discussions

- Summary
  - Make List of Control Signals for each Instruction
  - For each control signal, make List of Involved Instruction
  - Make Boolean Expression for each Control Signal
  - Make Micro-Program as Alternative Way of generating Control Signals

Summary and Further Discussions

- Additional Instruction

Instruction Type	Instructions
Data Transfer Instruction	Load, **LoadIndex**, Store, Move, Input, Ouput, **Movi, Storei, Outputi**
Data Operation Instruction	Neg, Abs, Inc, Dec, **Negi, Absi, Inci, Deci** Add, Sub, Arshift, Alshift AND, OR, XOR, Lrshift, Llshift
Control Transfer Instruction	Jump, Skip, Call, Return EQZBranch, NEQZBranch, GTZBranch LTZBranch **EQRBranch, NEQRBranch, GTRBranch LTRBranch** **EQVBranch, NEQVBranch, GTVBranch LTVBranch**

Summary and Further Discussions

- Added Operation Codes: Data Transfer Instruction

Op Prefix	Op Code	Instruction
00	0000 0000 0000	Move
00	0000 0000 0001	Load
00	0000 0000 0010	Store
00	0000 0000 0011	Input
00	0000 0000 0100	Output
00	0000 0000 0101	LoadIndex
00	0000 0000 0110	MovI
00	0000 0000 0111	StoreI
00	0000 0000 1000	OutputI

Summary and Further Discussions

- Hardware Implementation Modification

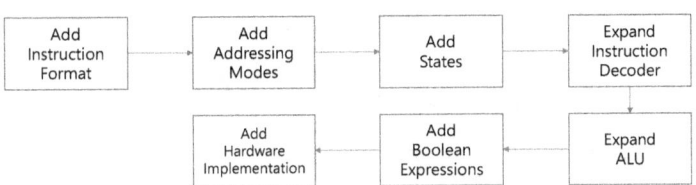

Control Signal = F(Added States, Added Instructions)

Summary and Further Discussions

- Added Micro-Instructions

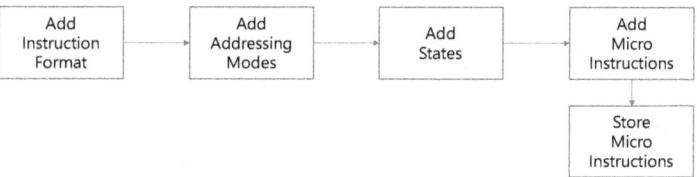